GRAMMAR MATTERS TOO

Michael Ross

With contributions from John Williams

Heinemann

CONTENTS

SECTION 4:
PARAGRAPHS AND WHOLE TEXTS

SECTION 5:
PUNCTUATION

SECTION 6:
COMMON ERRORS

SECTION 7:
APPLYING YOUR LEARNING

Introduction

Grammar Matters Too is a lively and informative Student Book that aims to improve your understanding and use of grammar.

This Student Book is clearly structured around units of work within larger sections. The book as a whole builds progression gradually through the introduction of familiar terms then new terms, and through the gradual introduction of increasing challenge. A variety of texts and examples are used with an emphasis on 'real-world' texts.

The features used in the Student Book are:

- **Objectives:** clearly stated at the beginning of each unit

- **Activities:** regular opportunities to practise and develop your skills through a variety of activity types

- **Did you know?:** provides a small piece of information related to that unit of work

- **Thinking back, moving forward:** offers the opportunity for self and peer assessment for each unit

- **Strategy:** offers tips for dealing with common errors.

Also available for Grammar Matters Too

Your teacher may also have the:

- **Teacher's Resource File** (together with a CD-ROM containing editable Word files of the TRF) that provides suggested answers to the activities in the Student Book plus a wealth of additional student worksheets and resources.

- **Interactive CD-ROM** that provides animations to bring the 'rules' of grammar alive together with interactive activities that match the contents of the Student Book and help appeal to different learning styles.

Introduction activity for students

If grammar could do this for you ...

1 Select your top three reasons from the box below for why you would *want* or *need* to learn about grammar.

2 Discuss your choices and compare them with other students' choices.

3 Do you have a reason that does not appear in the list below? If so, what is it?

- It helps you to speak fluently in a range of situations.
- You can persuade people more effectively of your point of view.
- You are able to write fluently for a range of audiences.
- You can understand some 'rules' of grammar.
- It makes your speaking and writing more interesting/original/powerful.
- You can avoid mistakes when you need to speak standard English.
- You can avoid mistakes when you need to write standard English.
- It is interesting to find out about how language works.
- It helps you to achieve higher grades in examinations.
- It helps you to get a job.
- It's good to be able to speak and write in a range of styles.
- Knowing how to use standard English gives you a wider choice of careers/jobs, etc.
- You are less likely to be misled by speakers and writers if you know the techniques they use.
- You can be more effective as a speaker if you know how language works.
- You can be more effective as a writer if you know how language works.
- It's interesting to be able to compare how English works with how other languages work.

I can highly recommend this!

WORDS AND PHRASES

Prefixes, stems and suffixes

OBJECTIVES

This unit will help you:

- understand how words are built up
- gain confidence in identifying prefixes, stems and suffixes
- gain confidence in spelling words by understanding their formation.

A **prefix** is a group of letters added to the *beginning* of a word.

A **suffix** is a group of letters added to the *end* of a word.

The **stem** is the group of letters *without* adding a prefix or suffix.

un	tie
prefix	**stem**

art	ist
stem	suffix

un	comfort	able
prefix	**stem**	suffix

Many words are made up of parts.
Read the following sentence.

Peter was very **disagreeable** on the way to the **supermarket**. It was **completely unnecessary**.

The words in bold can be broken down into parts.
Look at this table.

Prefix	Stem	Suffix
dis	agree	able
super	market	
	complete	ly
un	necessary	

Activity 1

Look at the words in bold in the paragraph below. Identify the stem and the prefix or suffix. The first one has been done for you in the table.

Prefix	Stem	Suffix
super	market	

> My mum drove us to the **supermarket** yesterday evening. At the roundabout there was a teenager on a **tricycle** going round **anticlockwise**! It was **remarkable** that she didn't have an accident. To my **amazement** she just rode off quite **unaware** of the trouble she had caused.

Using prefixes

A prefix can be added to the *beginning* of a stem to create a new word with a different meaning.

> The prefix **re-** means *again*.
> The word **start** means *to begin*.
> When you add **re-** to **start** you make the word **restart**.
> **Restart** means *to begin again*.

Activity 2

The prefix **un-** changes the meaning of the stem to its opposite. For example, something that is **safe** (not dangerous) would become **unsafe** (dangerous).

Write a sentence using one of the following stems with the prefix **un-**. For example: *I couldn't follow the instructions because they were unclear.*

friendly	sure	rehearsed	sympathetic

Activity 3

Make four words by matching each of the prefixes to the stems on the right. Then write a sentence for each word. Try to work out what each of the prefixes means.

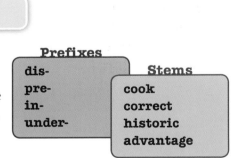

Prefixes
dis-
pre-
in-
under-

Stems
cook
correct
historic
advantage

Using suffixes

A suffix can be added to the *end* of a stem to create a new word.

Activity 4

1 Write a sentence using one of the following stems with the suffix **-ful**.

> care   help   pain   grace

2 Write a sentence using the stem you chose in question 1 with the suffix **-less**. What difference does adding this suffix make?

Activity 5

The suffixes **-ing** and **-ed** are two of the most commonly used suffixes in the English language.

1 Using the stem **help**, write a sentence using each of the following suffixes.
- **-ed**
- **-ing**

2 Using the stem **dance**, write a sentence using the following suffixes.
- **-ed**
- **-ing** (watch your spelling!)

3 Think of two more words that end in **-ed** and two more words that end in **-ing**. Write a sentence for each of the words you come up with.

Activity 6

Make as many words as you can from the following stems and suffixes. Then, write a sentence for each word you make.

Prefixes
play
entertain
modern
refresh
tidy
loud

Stems
-ment
-ful
-ly
-ness
-ing
-ize

Using stems, prefixes and suffixes

Words can be built using both prefixes and suffixes.
For example: **disappearance**. Prefixes and suffixes are
powerful because you can create many words from just
a few stems.

Activity 7

See how many words you can create by using the stems,
prefixes and suffixes below. Watch your spelling!

Prefix	Stem	Suffix
dis-	agree	-ity
in-	happy	-ly
re-	sincere	-ment
un-	turn	-ness
		-able

Activity 8

The sentences below do not make sense because the stems
in brackets are missing prefixes, suffixes or both. Work out
what the complete word should be for each of these stems,
then rewrite the sentences so that they make sense.

1 Our class studied (**globe**) (**warm**) today.
2 (**Fortunate**), we left the cake in the oven for too long
  and it didn't cook (**proper**).
3 Helen couldn't hide her (**excite**) when she (**cover**) the
  truth.
4 On our (**arrive**), the dog (**immediate**) ran to the door.
5 Our (**teach**) told me to (**simple**) my diagram, but
  I thought it was (**amaze**).
6 The floor was really (**dirt**) but we set about cleaning it
  (**energetic**).

Thinking back, moving forward

With your partner

Explain to each other:

— what a stem is

— what a suffix is and how you can use suffixes

— what a prefix is and how you can use prefixes.

On your own

How confident are you now that you can:

— identify prefixes, suffixes and stems

— spell words when you understand
  their formation?

Nouns

OBJECTIVES

This unit will help you:

- gain confidence in identifying different types of noun
- make your writing more precise by choosing the right noun
- use your knowledge of suffixes to spell nouns correctly.

What is a noun?

Nouns are words that name people, places, things, activities and states. If you ask a *who* or a *what* question, the answer will usually be a noun.

1. He takes their **dog** for a **walk** before **breakfast** every **day**.
2. **Ahmed's** favourite **sport** is **football**.
3. I had more **enjoyment** from a **part** in that **play** than anything else.
4. The **coach** expressed his **feelings** very clearly.
5. The **pitch** the **students** usually used between **lessons** was flooded.

People	Places	Things	Activities	States
Ahmed	pitch	dog	walk	enjoyment
coach		breakfast	sport	feelings
students		day	football	
		part	play	
		lessons		

Activity 1

Find the nouns in the following paragraph, then place them in a table like the one below. Decide which heading you think each noun fits best.

In this centre you can discover the magnificent world of the ocean. Visitors can have a close-up view of sharks, turtles and seahorses. There are interactive games in every room. Enjoyment is guaranteed!

People	Places	Things	Activities	States

Activity 2

Write three or four sentences on what you like to do at the weekend. Then underline each noun you use. Remember, you should underline any references to people, places, things, activities or states. For example:

> On <u>Saturdays</u>, I like to go to the <u>cinema</u> with my best <u>friend</u> <u>David</u>.

Do not underline words such as I, me, he, she and we (pronouns). These are covered in the next section (pages 18–23).

Plural nouns

The suffixes **-s** and **-es** are two of the most common suffixes in the English language. Most plurals are formed using one of these two suffixes.

Read the following rules on how to make nouns plural.

For most nouns add -**s**: bottle**s**, student**s**, book**s**
For nouns that end in **s, ss, x, z, ch, sh**, just add **es**:
 dress**es**, wish**es**

For nouns that end in **y**:
- add -**s** if the letter before **y** is *a, e, i, o, u*: toy**s**, day**s**
- change the **y** to **i** before adding -**es** if the letter before **y** is a consonant:
 body → bod**ies**

For nouns that end in **f** or **fe**, change the **f** to **v** before adding -**es or -s**:
 loaf → loa**ves**
 knife → kni**ves**

Exceptions
- For nouns ending in **ff** add -**s**: cliff**s**
- For some nouns ending in **f** or **fe**, add -**s**, e.g: reef**s**, brief**s**, fife**s**.

For nouns ending in **o** the suffix can be -**s** or -**es**:
 radio → radio**s**
 hero → hero**es**
Use a dictionary if you are not sure which suffix to use.

Activity 3

Look at the nouns in brackets in the following sentences. Write down their plural forms.

1 (**Baby**) enjoy hearing (**story**) read to them.
2 The (**hero**) of the (**book**) were police (**chief**).
3 Close up (**photo**) of (**mosquito**) show how they bite.
4 Most successful (**participant**) in (**quiz**) have a few good (**guess**).
5 Some (**newspaper**) like to report on the (**life**) of the (**wife**) of football (**player**).
6 The (**thief**) stole all the (**loaf**) from the local supermarket (**branch**).

There are some nouns that don't fit the rules for plurals listed on page 11. Some of these are very common words.

Activity 4

Each of the sentences below shows *one particular way* of forming a plural noun. Write down the plural forms of the nouns in brackets. Then, identify how the plurals are made in each sentence.

1 The (**woman**) and (**man**) were playing with their (**child**).
2 The (**mouse**) were chasing the (**louse**).
3 The (**goose**) were eating the bread at our (**foot**).
4 There are no (**formula**) for the number of (**antenna**) and (**vertebra**) in animals.
5 What (**criterion**) are used to tell the difference between normal events and strange (**phenomenon**)?

Now have a go at this one. (If you need help you can use a dictionary.)

6 There are many different (**species**) of (**deer**) and (**sheep**).

Proper nouns

Nouns can be broken down into different types.
Proper nouns are the names of *particular* people, places or things. They always start with a capital letter – for example, Laura, Hong Kong, Wednesday, *The Times*.

Activity 5

1 The following table shows some categories of proper nouns. Match the proper nouns below to the correct category in a table like the one below.

2 For each category, write two more examples of proper nouns.

Category	Proper noun
Country, nationality and/or language	
Town or city	
Name of person	
Religion	
Brand names	
Organisations	
Calendar days, months and holidays	

Australia	Hinduism
Pepsi	Oxfam
Bath	Nike
Edinburgh	Doctor Jones
Japanese	Jamie Oliver
Halloween	Christianity
September	Royal Mail

Activity 6

Proper nouns will be used particularly in geography and history lessons when writing about people, places and events.

Write down five proper nouns you would expect to use in each subject. Think of different types of place for geography, and try to include people, places and events for history. For example:

Geography – Asia, River Thames

History – Napoleon, First World War

Common nouns

Nouns that don't refer to particular people, places and things are **common nouns**. Common nouns can be divided into **count nouns** and **non-count nouns**.

Count nouns and non-count nouns

A **count noun** is a noun that has a plural form. It also refers to something you can count the number of. For example, if someone gave you some **coins** and asked you to count how many there were, you could count them.

A **non-count noun** is a noun that doesn't have a plural form. It also refers to something you can't count the number of. For example, it wouldn't make sense if you asked someone how many 'musics' they had. The word **music** doesn't have a plural form.

Activity

The following words are either count nouns or non-count nouns.

advice	anger	beef	book	bread
butter	computer	cow	egg	example
excitement	hay	luck	remark	tennis

Place them in the correct columns of a table like the one below. One has been done for you.

Count nouns	Non-count nouns
egg	

Fewer or less?

Read the following rules for using standard English.

- Use the word **fewer** when you are writing about a **count noun**. For example, *There are fewer **people** in my class today.*

- Use the word **less** when you are writing about a **non-count noun**. For example, *I'm having less **homework** this week.*

Activity 8

For each of the following words, write a sentence that correctly uses the words **less** or **fewer**. Remember to use the rules for count and non-count nouns.

- cars
- money
- problems
- rabbits
- traffic

Much or many?

Now read these rules.

- Use the word **many** when you are writing about a **count noun**. For example, *There were not **many** people at the party*.

- Use the word **much** when you are writing about a non-count noun. For example, *There was not **much** excitement at the party*.

Activity 9

Using the words in Activity 8, write a sentence that correctly uses the words **much** or **many**.

Using nouns in your writing

Activity 10

Look at the following sentences.

'You'll just have to trust me,' he said with a smile.

'You'll just have to trust me,' he said with a grin.

'You'll just have to trust me,' he said with a smirk.

The choice of *smile*, *grin* or *smirk* changes the way you think about the person. Discuss what difference you think it makes. You could also discuss which person you would trust most and which would you trust least.

Activity 11

The following newspaper article is about shops that are using 'Mosquito' devices to put off young people. (A 'Mosquito' is a device that sends out very high-pitched sounds that only young people can hear.)

1 Complete the article using the choice of nouns below. Note that your choice of noun will affect the reader's view of young people.

areas	yobs
shops	mobs
stores	nation
streets	youths
youngsters	country
corner-shops	avenues
gangs of youths	

2 Based on your choices, discuss what attitude the reader is encouraged to have of young people.

Why ▨ buzz off when they hear the sound of a Mosquito

For years the hooded ▨ of Britain have been free to roam the ▨'s shopping ▨. In the evenings and at the weekend they have loitered outside the ▨ of their choice.

Noun phrases

A **noun phrase** is a group of words built up on a noun. We add words before and after the noun to give more information. Look how a noun phrase is built below.

		teachers			
	some	**teachers**			
	some	**teachers**	at	our	school
some	English	**teachers**	at	our	school

Activity 12

Write out these sentences, turning the nouns in **bold** into noun phrases. There are words in the box below to help you.

The waiter slipped on _____ **floor**

and _____ **food** flew through the air.

We saw _____ **trifle** land on _____ **woman**.

| the tray of freshly-prepared | bits of |
| the hysterical | the newly-mopped |

Nouns and suffixes

Some suffixes are very commonly used in the formation of nouns.

Activity 13

Choose the suffix **-ity, -ment** or **-ion/-tion** to form nouns from the following words. Note down patterns you find in any spelling changes you have to make.

argue	active	advertise	agile	promote
assess	conclude	create	decide	develop
engage	explain	moral	persuade	real

Thinking back, moving forward

With your partner

Explain to each other:

- how to recognise a noun
- the different types of noun.

On your own

How confident are you now that you can:

- identify different types of noun
- make your writing more precise by choosing the right noun
- identify typical suffixes used to form nouns?

Pronouns

OBJECTIVES

This unit will help you:

- use pronouns in your writing
- use pronouns for particular effects
- avoid mistakes in using pronouns.

What is a pronoun?

A **pronoun** is a word that can replace a noun. If we didn't have pronouns, our writing would sound very repetitive.

> **Vicky** wondered if **Vicky** would make it in time for class.

Pronouns allow our writing to flow more easily.

> **Vicky** wondered if **she** would make it in time for class.

Activity 1

Make the following sentences sound less repetitive. Write out each sentence replacing one or more of the nouns with another word.

1 Alice turned off the television because Alice was bored with what was on.

2 Wayne had scored three goals so Wayne was made Man of the Match.

3 Pete and Ellie couldn't understand how Pete and Ellie had lost the quiz.

4 You can recycle plastic and cardboard by placing plastic and cardboard in the recycling bin.

The words you used in Activity 1 are examples of pronouns. You can use a pronoun instead of a noun when it is clear to the reader *who* or *what* you are writing about.

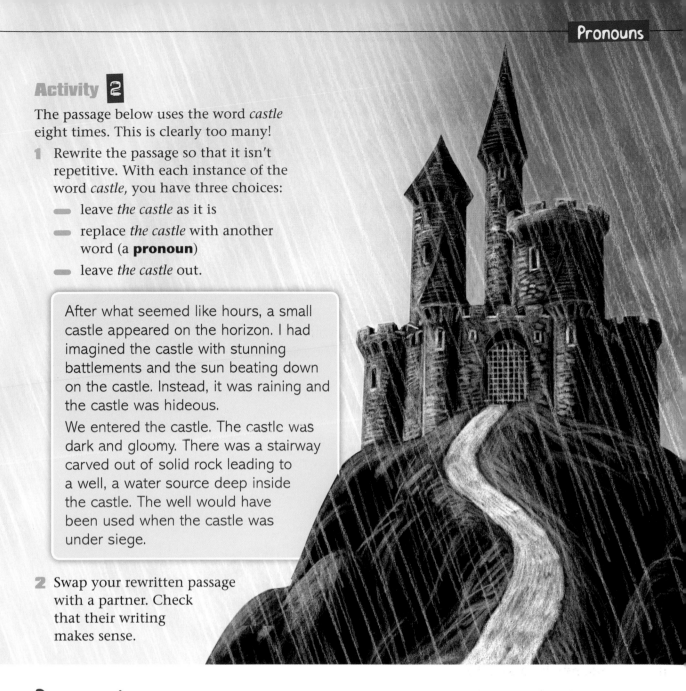

Activity 2

The passage below uses the word *castle* eight times. This is clearly too many!

1 Rewrite the passage so that it isn't repetitive. With each instance of the word *castle,* you have three choices:

— leave *the castle* as it is

— replace *the castle* with another word (a **pronoun**)

— leave *the castle* out.

> After what seemed like hours, a small castle appeared on the horizon. I had imagined the castle with stunning battlements and the sun beating down on the castle. Instead, it was raining and the castle was hideous.
>
> We entered the castle. The castle was dark and gloomy. There was a stairway carved out of solid rock leading to a well, a water source deep inside the castle. The well would have been used when the castle was under siege.

2 Swap your rewritten passage with a partner. Check that their writing makes sense.

Personal pronouns

Personal pronouns stand for people, places or things. The personal pronouns regularly used in speech and writing are shown in the table below.

	Subject	Object	
First person	I	me	
Second person	you	you	singular
Third person	she/he/it/one	her/him/it	
First person	we	us	
Second person	you	you	plural
Third person	they	them	

Activity 3

For each of the sentences below, select a suitable personal pronoun from the table on page 19. In most of the sentences you have a number of choices. Try to use a different pronoun each time.

1 _____ heard the news today.

2 _____ should have listened to my advice.

3 _____ opened the letter, hoping for good news.

4 She told _____ the news.

5 The teacher recommended _____ for an award.

6 The manager used _____ as a substitute striker.

Notice that in Activity 3, all the pronouns you used for 1–3 came from the **Subject** list, and all the pronouns you used for 4–6 came from the **Object** list.

Possessive pronouns

Possessive pronouns show who or what owns something. For example:

You know that's not **yours** – it's **mine**.

Both **yours** and **mine** are possessive pronouns.

	Singular	Plural
First person	mine	ours
Second person	yours	yours
Third person	his/hers/its	theirs

Activity 4

For each of the following sentences, replace the text in brackets with the correct possessive pronoun.

1 That's not your book, it's (**my book**).

2 You've had your meal. Now it's time for (**our meal**).

3 This is Daniel's T-shirt. (**Sarah's T-shirt**) is still in the washing machine.

4 My team won last night. (**Your team**) lost.

5 Our bus has arrived. (**The bus for them**) will arrive very soon.

Recognising pronouns

Read the extract from the back of a crisp packet. List all the pronouns, then decide what noun each pronoun has replaced.

When Angela started baking crisps 50 years ago, she wanted to make the best possible flavours. We have carried on this goal with Angela's Crisps, made only with the finest natural ingredients. We know that when you buy them, you will taste the quality.

First person or third person?

When you are writing a story, you can decide to write in the first person, using the pronoun **I**. This may be because it actually happened to you, or because you are imagining events from that person's point of view. You may also choose to write in the third person, using the pronouns **he** or **she**.

Activity 6

1 Change the following passage from third person to first person.

2 Which version do you think is more effective and why?

> Ann switched the light on, dreading what she knew she would see. The vase her mum had got for her 40th birthday from Ann's nan was shattered into a million pieces. Kirsty and Ann looked at each other in horror. No one else seemed all that bothered. Ann attempted to sweep it up, but the feeling of dread was growing.

Starting sentences with a pronoun

If a story starts with a line such as:

> *It couldn't have come at a worse time.*

or if a newspaper report starts with:

> *He played the game of his life yesterday.*

or if a music review starts with:

> *They have finally arrived with their latest recording …*

… the reader may well be intrigued. (What couldn't have come at a worse time? Who is the successful player? Which band has won praise for their latest recording?)

Activity 7

1 Write an opening sentence to a story in which you withhold information by using a pronoun. For example, you might not give away (until later) the *name of a character, what happened* or maybe *where something happened.*

2 Write a second sentence that reveals who or what the pronoun is referring to.

3 Discuss your sentences with a partner and be ready to share your example with the whole class.

What can go wrong with pronouns?

Activity 8

Read the following paragraph.

> Frank and Julia were reading in the garden. Their son John was mowing the lawn. He closed his book and asked him if he would like a drink. He said that was just what he needed, so he put his book down and made the drinks. When he returned, he and Julia were holding bags of grass. They put them down and Frank gave them them.

This paragraph contains too many pronouns. It isn't always clear who or what is being referred to. Change some of the pronouns in the paragraph so it is clear to the reader what is happening.

Pronouns and noun phrases

A **noun phrase** is a group of words built up on a noun. You can work out which part of a sentence is the noun phrase by trying to replace it with a pronoun. Look at the sentence below. Which words can be replaced by the pronoun **it**?

> I can't find my favourite CD.

Activity 9

Write out the following sentences and underline the exact part of the sentence that can be replaced by one of the pronouns below. Make a note of which pronoun you use in each case.

they	it	them

1 The blazing hot sun forced me to slow down.
2 I lost my favourite trainers.
3 The books that I borrowed from the library were due back today.
4 We watched the large crashing waves.
5 I accidentally knocked the blue vase over.

Thinking back, moving forward

With your partner
- Select what you think are the main mistakes you (or your class) make with pronouns.
- Prepare advice for someone who makes these mistakes.

On your own
How confident are you now that you can:
- recognise a pronoun and identify different types
- withhold information using pronouns
- vary your writing by using pronouns in different ways?

Adjectives

This unit will help you:

- use a range of adjectives in your writing
- use comparative and superlative adjectives effectively
- use your knowledge of suffixes to spell adjectives correctly.

Adjectives

Adjectives are often called 'describing words' because they give us more information about nouns. Look at the adjectives (in **bold**) in the following passage. They describe the cat, the house, the windows and the garden.

> The **black** cat with the **shining**, **green** eyes sat in front of the **strange** house. The house appeared **old** and **dark** with **large**, **gloomy** windows and an **overgrown** garden.

Adjectives can be used in two ways.

1 They can be placed before the noun:

> ... **shining**, **green** eyes

2 They can be placed after certain verbs such as *seem*, *be* and *appear*:

> The house appeared **old** and **dark**.

Adjectives also appear in a certain order:

A **fantastic**, big, **red** bus

opinion   size/density   colour

Activity 1

Find the adjectives in the passage below and write them down.

> The dark and gloomy atmosphere disappeared when the large black door swung open. Brilliant golden sunlight struck the grand reading-room. The old wooden shelves stood tall and elegant, lined with hundreds of antique books.

Activity 2

Use adjectives to fill in the spaces on the postcard.

We're having a _____ time, although the weather's been _____. The sea was just _____ enough for me to stay in for a _____ swim, and Mark's been doing some surfing, which he says was _____. There was _____ rain on Sunday, but we spent our time in a _____ place called Techniquest.

James Arnold
23 Acacia Avenue
Northton
England

Activity 3

1 An advertising agency has come up with an advertisement to promote a new fruit smoothie. However, there are some gaps in the text. Fill in the gaps by choosing from the adjectives provided so that the readers will want to buy the smoothie.

fresh fruit smoothies

Start your day with our _____, _____ breakfast smoothies.
Made from _____ fruit, our smoothies are the most _____ way to start your day.

delicious	health-boosting	disgusting	natural	tasty
rotten	unhealthy	unwholesome	artificial	mouth-watering
yummy	nutritious	nourishing	wholesome	fresh
old	tasteless	fulfilling		

2 How did you decide which adjectives to use for this advertisement?

Activity 4

1 Write three sentences describing a real or imaginary person, then underline the adjectives. Think carefully about the adjectives you use. Try to:
- use two or three adjectives together
- place adjectives before the noun and after verbs like *be* and *seem*.

For example:

> My **six-year-old** niece is **boisterous** and **loud**! She has **sparkling**, **chocolate-coloured** eyes and **crazy**, **brown** curls.

You could use the adjectives below as a starting point.

hair: cropped, braided, wavy, dyed

eyes: blue, hazel, beady, piercing

personality: friendly, witty, nervous, bubbly

2 When you hear some descriptions read out, decide which you think is the best and why.
- Be prepared to explain to others what makes it effective.
- Note down any ideas you could use in your own descriptions to make them more interesting.

Activity 5

Here is part of a description written by a student.
The adjectives are in **bold**.

1 What is best about the student's use of adjectives here and why? For example, what can you picture?

2 If you were to suggest an improvement, what would it be and why?

> Outside the slightly **grimy** windows and past the **cheap, red**, couch, it's **baking**. A family, with a **small** boy hanging onto the man's arm and the woman pushing a pushchair, are struggling through the **swinging** doors. A **teenage** girl with **black** hair in pigtails holds one of the doors open for them, and the woman smiles gratefully.

Comparative and superlative adjectives

Comparative adjectives are used when we *compare one thing with another*. For example, you can use a comparative adjective to compare the temperature between two days.

> It is **colder** today than yesterday.
> It is **less cold** today than yesterday.

Superlative adjectives are used when we *compare more than two things*. So you can use a superlative adjective to compare the temperature when you are comparing three or more days.

> Today is the **coldest** day of the week.
> Today is the **least cold** day of the week.

For comparison to a **lower degree**, simply use **less** and **least**:

tidy → **less** tidy → **least** tidy

For comparison to a **higher degree**, do the following.

Note that the following is a guide. There are exceptions, some of which are noted at the bottom.

If the adjective has one syllable:

- Make the comparative form by adding -**er** to the adjective.
- Make the superlative form by adding -**est** to the adjective.

small → small**er** → small**est**

If the adjective has more than two syllables:

- Make the comparative form by placing the word **more** in front of the adjective.
- Make the superlative form by placing the word **most** in front of the adjective.

exciting → **more** exciting → **most** exciting

If the adjective has exactly two syllables:

The comparative and superlative adjectives are sometimes formed with -**er** and -**est**, sometimes with **more** and **most**, and sometimes either way.

quiet → quiet**er** → quiet**est**

quiet → **more** quiet → **most** quiet

There are some exceptions to the rules

good → better → best

bad → worse → worst

little → less → least

many → more → most

Activity 6

Identify the comparative and superlative adjectives in these sentences.

1 Faster than a shuttle take-off, speedier than a Ferrari and with more lift than a plane, this rollercoaster will blow your mind!

2 The UK's most thrilling theme park! It has Europe's fastest and tallest rollercoaster.

Activity 7

Replace the adjectives in brackets with the correct **comparative** form.

1 My old bedroom was (**small**) than the one I'm in now.

2 His spelling is (**accurate**) than mine.

3 Be (**strict**) when training your dog.

4 The book was (**interesting**) than I thought.

5 The new building was (**spacious**).

Activity 8

Replace the adjectives in brackets with the correct **superlative** form.

1 It was the (**bad**) meal I had ever eaten.

2 The final book in the trilogy was by far the (**good**).

3 That was the (**exciting**) game I have ever watched.

4 They were the (**narrow**) lanes I've had to cycle through.

5 Waiting at the airport was the (**mind-numbing**) experience I have ever had.

Advertisers often use superlative adjectives in their advertisements because they like to suggest that you will get the best if you buy their product.

Activity 9

You have been asked by a sports company to design an advertisement for 'Trailblazers', a new brand of trainers for 12 to 15-year-olds. The company wants you to present this brand of trainers as the *best*. Make notes for your advertisement, thinking about the following features: style, comfort, range of colours and cost.

Turning nouns into adjectives

Some nouns can be turned into adjectives by adding a suffix to them. For example:

hero + **ic** = hero**ic**

Activity 10

1 Using a suffix at the end of the following words will change the noun to an adjective. What is the suffix you can use in all six examples?

2 Write a rule for how to spell words using this suffix.

> agriculture   music   nation   nature   person

Turning verbs into adjectives

Some verbs can be turned into adjectives by adding a suffix to them. For example:

wash + **able** = wash**able**

Activity 11

1 Change the following verbs into adjectives by adding the suffix -**ing**.

2 Work out the rules for changing verbs into adjectives using the suffix -**ing**.

> amaze   astonish   depress   enchant
> excite   intrigue   mislead   tempt

DID YOU KNOW?

There is an adjective in English that has two different spellings:

- **blond** when you are referring to males
- **blonde** when you are referring to females.

Thinking back, moving forward

With your partner

Explain to each other:

- how to form adjectives when you are comparing things in your writing
- how to vary your sentences by using adjectives in different ways.

On your own

How confident are you now that you can:

- use a range of adjectives
- use comparative and superlative adjectives effectively
- use your knowledge of suffixes to spell adjectives correctly?

Verbs

OBJECTIVES

This unit will help you:

— gain confidence in identifying verbs and verb phrases

— use verbs to express past, present and future time

— make your writing more precise by choosing the right verb

— recognise common prefixes and suffixes that are used to form verbs.

What is a verb?

The answer to the following questions will usually be a **verb**.

— What is happening?

— What are you doing?

A word is a **verb** if it:

— represents an **action**	to **run**, to **shake**, to **read**, to **take**
— represents **speech**	to **say**, to **explain**, to **promise**, to **tell**
— represents **senses**	to **think**, to **feel**, to **enjoy**, to **taste**

Some verbs are used to link two parts of a sentence:

— That **was** our new teacher.

— This **is** a sentence.

Activity 1

Write down the **verb** in each of the following sentences.

1 On Saturday, Yasmeen went to the bookshop.

2 The bookshop was always busy on a Saturday.

3 The shop assistant smiled at Yasmeen from behind the counter.

4 Yasmeen asked the shop assistant for a particular book.

5 The shop assistant had a good knowledge of the bookshop.

DID YOU KNOW?

When the word '**to**' sits in front of a verb, the verb is in its 'infinitive form'.

Activity 2

Write down a **verb** for each of the sentences below.

1 Joe _____ what it is like to be a famous footballer.

2 My brother _____ the drums for a rock band.

3 It _____ a really good film.

4 Climbing is what Stacey _____ to do at the weekend.

5 I sometimes wish we _____ more sunshine.

The verbs you use can vary the way a person or situation is shown. Look at the three sentences below.

> Mr Bolton **walked** into the classroom.
> Mr Bolton **stormed** into the classroom.
> Mr Bolton **strolled** into the classroom.

Each of the verbs above gives a very different picture of how Mr Bolton entered the classroom.

Activity 3

The following passage is about a baker serving a customer. Rewrite the passage choosing the **verbs** in the word bank below. Write the following:

- one version where the baker and the customer are very grumpy
- one version where the baker and the customer are friendly and polite.

> Mrs Green _____ into the bakery and _____ the door. The baker _____ at Mrs Green and _____, 'What would you like?'
>   Mrs Green _____, 'Three fruit scones.'
>   The baker _____ the fruit scones into a paper bag, and Mrs Green _____ the money on the counter.

strolled	stormed	walked	slammed
closed	smiled	glared	frowned
asked	barked	screeched	replied
put	threw	placed	banged

Verb phrases

Verbs can be more than just a single word. Look at the paragraph below. It contains **verb phrases** that are one word and more than one word (shown in **bold**).

> I **had been planning** a visit to the park today but then the rain **started**. I **did have** an umbrella but it **was raining** heavily. So I **decided** that instead I **would play** on my computer. I **might go** to the park tomorrow.

Look at the following **verb phrase**. It has a **main verb**.

> I might **go** to the park tomorrow.
>
> O 'go' is the main verb. It is the main thing being done.

The other verb in the verb phrase is an **auxiliary verb**.

> I **might** go to the park tomorrow.
>
> O 'might' is the auxiliary verb. It comes before the main verb and changes the meaning of the verb phrase.

Some verb phrases have more than one auxiliary verb.

> I **had** been **planning** a visit to the park today.
>
> O auxiliary verb   O auxiliary verb   O main verb

Activity 4

Write down the **verb phrase** in each of the sentences below. Try to make sure you find all of the words that form the verb phrase.

1 You can join the team.

2 I will write my postcards tomorrow.

3 Hannah might leave the party early.

4 Chris has tidied his bedroom.

5 I may finish the book before you.

6 I do know the rules of football.

7 My friend has moved to a different class.

8 The band was playing well.

9 I could have solved that puzzle.

10 Mrs Tulip could have been our teacher.

Activity 5

For each verb phrase you wrote down in Activity 4, make a table like the one below to show auxiliary verbs and the main verb. There must be a main verb for each sentence. The first one has been done for you

Verb phrase	Auxiliary verb/s	Main verb
can join	can	join

Modal auxiliary verbs

Modal verbs are a type of auxiliary verb. They are used to 'help' other verbs express a meaning. In particular, they show **degrees of certainty**.

I **could** eat spinach.
I **should** eat spinach.
I **must** eat spinach.
I **will** eat spinach.

The following are also modal auxiliary verbs.

can	**may**	**might**
ought to	**shall**	**would**

Activity 6

Write out the following passage, filling in the gaps with **modal auxiliary verbs.**

I _____ go to see that film this weekend.
I _____ look on the internet and see if there
are any reviews. That _____ tell me if it's worth
watching. If I do see a good review, I _____ text
you and we _____ go to the cinema together.

The verbs in a verb phrase do not always sit next to each other. Look at the following sentences.

> **Can** you **talk** more quietly please?
>
> I **will** soon **make** some big changes.

Activity 7

Write down the **verb phrases** in the following sentences.

1 Would you like some orange juice?

2 I have already watched that film.

3 Could we go somewhere else?

4 I had completely forgotten that.

Verbs and time

We can use verbs to show when something is happening in the **past**, **present** or **future**.

He **kicked** the ball into the back of the net.	(refers to the **past**)
He **kicks** the ball into the back of the net.	(refers to the **present**)
He **likes** football.	(refers to the **present**)
He **will kick** the ball into the back of the net.	(refers to the **future**)

Activity 8

Write down whether the following sentences are referring to **past**, **present** or **future** time.

1 Gemma **throws** the ball to Sandy.

2 I **will go** shopping with Dad.

3 I **was** happy about being selected for the team.

4 I **left** for school as the downpour started.

5 The Earth **travels** around the Sun.

6 They **stayed** in the park all day.

7 Ray **is playing** on his computer.

8 My father **teaches** in a secondary school.

You can change the time referred to in your writing by changing the verbs.

Activity 9

1 Change the following passage so that it refers to the present. Note: you do not need to change *all* the verbs. Record the changes you have made.

> Alton Towers was full of children. There were children everywhere. Everywhere you looked there was an overexcited child screaming happily with the thought of all the fun contained in one park. The sweet stalls, covered in bags of candyfloss and other such brightly-coloured delights, were heaving with hordes of sweet-toothed children. The ornament stalls were also packed.

2 Select one time when you decided *not* to change a word ending in **-ed** and explain why.

3 Explain which version you think is more effective as a piece of writing and why.

Some writers make the mistake of switching between the past and the present in their writing. When writing, you need to make sure that you don't confuse the time.

Activity 10

The passage on the right was written by a student. In this piece of writing, the time has been muddled. Rewrite the passage so that the time referred to is consistent.

- Imagine the party happened some time ago.
- You will need to change some words in addition to verbs.

> Everyone was expecting me to have a party. But I haven't even asked my mum yet. I thought she will probably say yes so I decide I will ask her tonight.
>
> I was going to invite my two best friends: Mandy and Suzy. I decide I will tell them about the party tomorrow.

Choosing powerful verbs

Activity 11

The following extract is taken from *Stormbreaker* by Anthony Horowitz.

With a partner, replace the verbs in **bold** with your choice from the actual verbs used by Anthony Horowitz (given in the word box). Then, discuss the effect of the change in each case.

> The operator – sitting in a glass cabin at one end of the crusher – **pushed** a button and there was a great belch of black smoke. The shelves **shut** on the car like a monster insect folding in its wings. There was a grinding sound as the car **was pressed** until it was no bigger than a rolled-up carpet. Then the operator **changed** a gear and the car **was pushed** out, metallic toothpaste **being cut up** by a hidden blade. The slices **fell** to the ground.

being chopped up	closed in	pressed	threw
tumbled on	was crushed	was squeezed	

Understanding how verbs are formed

Suffixes can be added to the end of a word to change that word in some way. Look at these examples.

> Add the suffix -**ed** to change **ask** to **asked**.
>   → I only ask**ed**.
> Add the suffix -**ing** to change **ask** to **asking**
>   → I was only ask**ing**.

Activity 12

1 Change the form of the following verbs by adding the suffixes -**ed** and -**ing**.

2 Prepare advice for someone who tends to make mistakes when spelling these words.

allow	believe	brake	manage
deny	climb	happen	listen

Prefixes can be added to the beginning of a verb to change its meaning in some way. Look at these examples.

Add the prefix **mis**- to change **lead** to **mislead**

Add the prefix **re**- to change **assure** to **reassure**

Activity 13

Create different verbs by adding one or more of the following prefixes to the verbs. Make a note in the box of any subject area in which you might use the new word.

Prefixes	Verbs
dis-	appear
photo-	appoint
pre-	assemble
re-	copy
	search
	view

Thinking back, moving forward

With your partner

— Explain how you can vary your verb phrases by using auxiliary verbs.

— Discuss how prefixes and suffixes can help you with the spelling and meaning of verbs.

On your own

How confident are you now that you can:

— identify verbs and verb phrases

— use verbs to express past, present and future time

— make your writing more precise by choosing the right verb

— recognise common prefixes and suffixes that are used to form verbs?

Adverbs

OBJECTIVES

I can highly recommend this!

This unit will help you:

— identify an adverb

— gain confidence in choosing adverbs for your writing

— vary the way that you use adverbs in your writing.

What is an adverb?

Adverbs are words that answer the following questions.

How?

Natalie ran **quickly**.　　(**How** did Natalie run?)
Simon sang **loudly**.　　(**How** did Simon sing?)

When?

We are playing football **tomorrow**.　(**When** are you playing football?)
Afterwards we went camping.　　(**When** did you go camping?)

Where?

I left my book **there**.　　(**Where** did you leave your book?)
I am going **home**.　　(**Where** are you going?)

Warning – *there* and *home* are not always adverbs.
Check if they answer the question **Where**?

Adverbs give more information about *verbs*. For example:

Simon sang loudly.

verb ———●　　●——— The adverb tells us more about how Simon sang.

Adverbs also give more information about *adjectives*. For example:

Dad was extremely tired.

The adverb tells us more about how tired Dad was.　　adjective

Adverbs can also give more information about *adverbs*. For example:

Vashti told the joke very skilfully.

'very' tells us how skilfully　　'skilfully' tells us *how* Vashti told the joke.

Activity 1

Find the adverbs in the following sentences, then write them down.

1 Alex was waiting there.
2 Nadine thought carefully about the question.
3 We planned to meet today.
4 Charlotte sang confidently at the karaoke.
5 Kamal wrote his letter very neatly.

Activity 2

Write down the adverbs from the following paragraph. Look for **single words** that answer these questions: *How? When?* or *Where?* The first adverb is shown in **bold**.

… When he picked it up he **immediately** realised that here was a tin with a difference.

For one thing, it was lighter than all the others he had come across. Far, far lighter. This was definitely no ordinary tin of beans or soup or stewed steak or curried chicken or macaroni cheese. This was a tin which felt so light that it could almost have been empty. But despite being so light, it definitely had something inside it. Fergal knew that for certain. He could tell that quite clearly.

Extract from *Tins* by Alex Shearer

Activity 3

For each blank space in the passage below, choose an adverb from the word box that you think fits best.

I was _____ interested in the new music download system. _____ it was _____ easy to use, and you could _____ choose what you _____ wanted.

absolutely	amazingly	essentially	exactly
extremely	fundamentally	genuinely	instantly
particularly	specifically	really	very
quickly	basically	quite	

Where can an adverb go in a sentence?

If you always put an adverb in the same place in a sentence, it can make your writing seem repetitive. Read the following sentences.

> She put the key in the door **cautiously**. She entered the house **silently**. She picked up the post **excitedly**.

These sentences all sound the same. You can solve this by moving the adverb. Look at the following choices.

> **Cautiously**, she put the key in the door.
> She **cautiously** put the key in the door.
> She put the key in the door **cautiously**.

Activity 4

In the following passage, the adverbs are always at the end of the sentence. Rewrite the passage so that the adverbs are in different places in the sentences.

> The manager had agreed to hold the party in the function room enthusiastically. She walked towards the round table in the centre of the room cheerfully. She took orders quickly and efficiently. A party of twelve was already singing merrily.

Activity 5

Write down the adverbs in the following passage, and the words that those adverbs are giving information about. Use what you have learned so far about adverbs to help you. For example, the adverb 'sleepily' (shown in **bold**) shows *how* the writer 'got up from [his] bed'.

> I got up from my bed **sleepily**. Foolishly, I had left it too late as usual. I searched frantically for my school uniform, finding it eventually in various extremely strange places. After rapidly eating my breakfast, I left the house and ran to catch the bus.
>
> Curiously, the bus stop was unusually quiet. I suddenly realised the reason. It was a school closure day.

Adverbs in advertising

Advertisers regularly use adverbs to encourage the public to use their products. For example:

- We have an *excitingly* original range.
- We make *terrifically* tasty crisps.
- *Fantastically* generous offers are available today.
- You can be sure of a *thrillingly* exciting day.

Have you seen or heard other examples?

Activity 6

Decide on a product you are going to advertise such as a new drink, cereal bar or pair of trainers. Now write three sentences, with at least one adverb in each, advertising your product. Use what you have learned so far about adverbs to help you.

You could choose from this word box, or make your own choice.

amazingly	brilliantly
excellently	expertly
futuristically	safely
skilfully	specially
tastily	technically
wonderfully	
mouthwateringly	

Patterns for spelling adverbs

Typically, adverbs are formed by adding the suffix **-ly**. For example:

actual**ly** sincere**ly** skilful**ly** sure**ly** unfortunate**ly**

Activity 7

Not all adverbs can be formed by just adding **-ly**. For the following exceptions, note down what you need to do before adding the suffix **-ly**.

necessary → necessarily   terrible → terribly

true → truly   whole → wholly

Thinking back, moving forward

With your partner

- Explain how you can use adverbs at different points in a sentence and use them in different ways.
- Find a recent piece of writing that includes adverbs and exchange it with your partner. Give each other at least one piece of advice about how to improve it by using adverbs in a more interesting way.

On your own

How confident are you now that you can:

- identify an adverb
- vary the way that you use adverbs?

Prepositions

OBJECTIVES

This unit will help you:

- gain confidence in identifying prepositions
- use prepositions in your writing
- vary your sentence structures by changing the position of prepositions in your writing.

I'm on top of the world!

What is a preposition?

Prepositions are words that go before nouns, pronouns, and noun phrases. Prepositions provide information about:

Place		Time	
position	**on** the table	point in time	**at** midnight
origin	**from** Oxford	origin	**since** yesterday
direction	**towards** Cambridge	end point	**until** Monday
extent	**for** three kilometres	extent	**for** several minutes

Note: prepositions can also provide information about manner (**with** *great skill*)

Activity 1

Write out the following passage in full, using the words below it to fill in any gaps. The words below are a mixture of prepositions of place and time.

> My day started _____ 6 o'clock. I made some sandwiches _____ myself and collected my bike _____ the shed. I rode _____ school, avoiding the route _____ the dual carriageway and instead went _____ the bridge. I arrived just before the coach left, leaving my bike _____ the school office.

across	at	before	beside
for	from	over	to

The words that you have used to fill the gaps in Activity 1 are all prepositions.

Prepositions that show time

after	at	before	between	by
during	for	from	in	on
over	past	since	until	to

Activity 2

Write three sentences that show when something is happening. Each sentence should use one of the prepositions above with a choice of the words below. For example: **After** breakfast I brushed my teeth.

August	bedtime	breakfast	eight o'clock
lessons	lunchtime	May Day	night
Saturday	spring	the weekend	two weeks

Activity 3

Write three sentences to a friend or relative telling them about a day out or event that you liked. Underline each preposition of time that you use. For example: **After** the concert we went for a pizza.

Prepositions that show place

above	among	at	behind
below	beside	between	beyond
by	in	in front of	inside
next to	on	outside	under
from	to		

Activity 4

1 Write about a place you know well, such as your bedroom or your favourite space. Each sentence should begin with one of the prepositions in the box above. For example: **Behind** the door hangs my favourite top.

2 Now rewrite your sentences and change the position of some of the prepositions. For example: My favourite top hangs **behind** the door.

DID YOU KNOW?

Groups of words that begin with a preposition and are followed by a noun phrase are called **prepositional phrases**. For example:

after midnight
towards me
at high speed

They often answer the questions 'When?' 'Where?' or 'How?'

Prepositions that show movement

Activity 5

Write five sentences for a satellite navigation system, describing the route from your school to a surprise venue you have chosen for friends coming to an after-school party. Use at least one preposition of movement in each sentence (see the word box below).

You could include phrases such as: *past the garage*; *under the bridge*; *round the roundabout*; *across the traffic lights*.

across	along	around
back to	down	into
off	onto	out of
over	past	round
through	to	towards
up		
under		

Is this a preposition?

Activity 6

A word in the sign below is incorrect. With a partner, decide which word it is and what it should change to.

Thinking back, moving forward

With your partner

- Discuss how you could explain to someone when to use the word *past* and when to use the word *passed*.

- Decide where you could use each type of preposition most effectively in your writing.

On your own

How confident are you now that you can:

- identify different types of preposition

- use prepositions in your writing

- change the position of prepositions in your writing?

This unit will help you:

- gain confidence in identifying sentences
- use different kinds of sentences in your writing
- understand what a simple sentence is
- understand subject/verb agreement.

What is a sentence?

The rules

A written sentence **makes sense on its own** and usually:

has a verb,

starts with a capital letter,

and ends in a full stop, question mark or exclamation mark.

The following string of words is a sentence.

Capital letter   Verb   Full stop

The best athletes wear special trainers.

The whole sentence makes sense on its own.

Activity 1

Below are ten pieces of text from advertisements. Identify which ones are sentences, using the rules on page 48.

1 They are big and they are clever!

2 Dreamy white chocolate

3 Check out our new healthy range.

4 Milk chocolate with gold honeycomb centre

5 Do you dare to whizz, loop and twist on a journey of terror?

6 How about trying our spicy meat pizza?

7 Roly Poly Coaster

8 GO ROUND THE BEND!

9 Fly off the handle!

10 The crumbliest flakiest milk chocolate

Activity 2

Below are ten sentences. With a partner, take turns to explain why each one is a sentence. Remember the rules used for identifying sentences.

1 Everyone likes a challenge.
2 Use in a well ventilated area.
3 Enjoy!
4 Thousands of sports fans let out a miserable cheer yesterday.
5 We will match any price.
6 Repeat, please.
7 My side of the story is really simple.
8 Buy now!
9 On the morning of 25 February we left the city.
10 Win!

We can now identify groups of words as sentences by recognising the patterns that they follow. We will be looking at the patterns that different types of sentences make in the following units.

DID YOU KNOW?

It's possible to have really short sentences. Look at the sentences in Activity 2. There are sentences such as '**Win!**', '**Enjoy!**' and '**Buy now!**'

Kinds of sentence

Here are the four main kinds of sentence.

Statement   **Question**

Exclamation   **Command**

Statement This is the kind of sentence that is most common in writing:

We won the competition.

Question We use a question when we want to know the answer to something. Questions are punctuated with a question mark:

Did we win?

Exclamation Exclamations show strong emotions such as excitement, surprise or anger. They are punctuated with an exclamation mark.

What a noise!

Command We make a command when we want someone to do something.

Tell me what the result was.

DID YOU KNOW?

True exclamations have a special word order, e.g. 'What a wonderful day that was!' However, we often show exclamations by writing a statement followed by an exclamation mark, e.g. 'That was a wonderful day!'

DID YOU KNOW?

A **directive** is a sentence which instructs someone to do something. But it does not have to be a **command** or an **exclamation**. For example: *Have a nice day.*

Activity 1

1 Read the following extract from *George's Marvellous Medicine* by Roald Dahl. Identify the following:
   - four statements
   - four questions
   - four exclamations.
2 What do the questions and exclamations tell us about the relationship between Grandma, Mr Kranky and Mrs Kranky?
3 Imagine that the next thing George does is make a statement sentence. What might it be?

Grandma's tiny face still bore the same foul and furious expression it had always had. Her eyes, no bigger now than little keyholes, were blazing with anger. 'How do I feel?' she yelled. 'How d'you think I feel?'

How would you feel if you'd been a glorious giant a minute ago and suddenly you're a miserable midget?

'She's still going!' shouted Mr Kranky gleefully. 'She's still getting smaller!'

And by golly she was.

When she was no bigger than a cigarette, Mrs Kranky made a grab for her. She held her in her hands and she cried, 'How do I stop her from getting smaller still?'

'You can't,' said Mr Kranky. 'She's had fifty times the right amount.'

'I must stop her!' Mrs Kranky wailed. 'I can hardly see her as it is!'

'Catch hold of each end and pull,' Mr Kranky said.

By then, Grandma was the size of a matchstick and still shrinking fast.

A moment later, she was no bigger than a pin …

Then a pumpkin seed …

Then …

Then …

'Where is she?' cried Mrs Kranky. 'I've lost her!'

'Hooray,' said Mr Kranky.

'She's gone! She's disappeared completely!' cried Mrs Kranky.

'That's what happens to you if you're grumpy and bad-tempered,' said Mr Kranky. 'Great medicine of yours, George.'

George didn't know what to think.

For a few minutes, Mrs Kranky kept wandering round with a puzzled look on her face, saying, 'Mother, where are you? Where've you gone? Where've you got to? How can I find you?' But she calmed down quite quickly. And by lunchtime, she was saying, 'Ah well, I suppose it's all for the best, really. She was a bit of a nuisance around the house, wasn't she?'

'Yes,' replied Mr Kranky. 'She most certainly was.'

George didn't say a word. He felt quite trembly. He knew something tremendous had taken place that morning. For a few brief moments he had touched with the very tips of his fingers the edge of a magic world.

Activity 2

Work with a partner to write a newspaper article about the mystery of Grandma's disappearance. Be sure to include questions, statements, exclamations and commands.

Ideas to help: write as if you are the reporter but try to avoid using 'I' or 'me'. Include the setting, the police questioning of Mr and Mrs Kranky, and their astonished replies.

Simple sentences

What is a simple sentence?

Simple sentences are made up of just one clause. They must contain a **subject** and a **verb**.

Selma reads her *Spiderman* comic.

subject   verb

In addition, simple sentences can also have the following.

Object   **Complement**   **Adverbial**

We will look at each of these elements in more detail throughout this section. First, we will look at verbs.

Verb

A simple sentence has one **complete verb** or **verb phrase**. A verb phrase is the main verb plus any auxillary verbs. Look at the sentence below. The verb is in **bold**.

I **cooked** dinner for Chloe.

It is possible to take out parts of this sentence and still have a sentence that makes sense.

I **cooked** dinner.

I **cooked** for Chloe.

I **cooked**.

But if we take out the verb, it isn't a sentence anymore.

I dinner for Chloe.

Activity 1

Write three sentences, each using one *noun* or *pronoun* and one *verb* from the table below. Do not use the same noun or verb twice. Make sure your sentences make sense.

Noun/pronoun	Verb
The kite	meandered.
The river	flew.
I	galloped.
Dad	escaped.
The horse	laughed.

Activity 2

The following sentences are missing a **verb**. Think of verbs to fill the spaces, then write out the sentences in full. Remember that a verb or verb phrase can be more than one word.

1 The football players _____ onto the pitch.

2 The front door _____ slowly.

3 Ravi didn't _____ vampires were real.

4 The firework _____ in the sky.

5 The cottage _____ in snow.

6 The fans _____ loudly.

7 The firemen _____ the fire.

8 The book _____ really exciting.

Activity 3

Write two or three sentences about a simple scientific experiment you have done. This could be a scientific experiment at school, or another form of experiment or something imaginary. Then underline the **verb phrases**.

The subject

Simple sentences also have a **subject**. The subject is linked to the verb and shows us **who** or **what** the sentence is about.

> **Michelle** found the ticket.
> Yesterday **Tom** played in goal.
> **The magazine** lay on the floor.
> **The idea** came in a flash.

Activity 4

Write out the following sentences, then underline the **subject**.

1 The horse ran out of the stable.
2 Alice kicked the football.
3 The car reversed into the parking space.
4 London is a big city.
5 I accidentally threw the ball into the greenhouse.

Activity 5

The following sentences are missing a **subject**. Think of subjects to fill the spaces, then write out the sentences in full.

1 _____ was busy tidying the house.
2 _____ crashed onto the floor.
3 _____ wanted me to go to the cinema last night.
4 _____ blazed down on the desert.
5 _____ was playing really loudly.

Activity 6

In the following passage, the subjects are muddled. With a partner, find the correct place for each subject. Then write out the passage correctly.

> **The crowd** crossed the line in first place.
> **A trophy** cheered with delight. **Journalists** was given to the driver for his victory. **The driver** scrambled to get an interview with him.

Different subjects

Sometimes the subject can be the words 'there' or 'it'.

> **There** were lots of people at the party.
> **It** is not surprising that the party was a success.

You can also find subjects made up of more than one word.

> **Thousands of sports fans** let out a miserable
> cheer yesterday.

Sometimes the subject isn't at the beginning of the sentence.

> Is **Alison** playing volleyball with us tomorrow?
> Suddenly, **the fish** leaped out of the water.

Activity

Write down the **subjects** in the following passage.

> At the weekend we went to the Natural History Museum. There was plenty to
> see there. My favourite thing to visit was the dinosaur gallery. It was absolutely
> fascinating. All around there were lots of dinosaur skeletons. The Tyrannosaurus
> Rex's skeleton was gigantic! I bet it would have been terrifying to come across a
> real one. Now I can imagine what the people in *Jurassic Park* felt like!

Now let's try to identify both subjects and verbs.

Activity 8

Write out the following sentences. Then label the **subject** and
verb. Remember a subject and verb can both be more than
one word.

1 It is a really good film.
2 The thunder rumbled loudly.
3 I was expecting you to call.
4 Experiments in science lessons can be fun.
5 Some television programmes are really interesting.
6 Neither Lucy nor Fiona plays the clarinet.
7 The footballer who played in all the matches won the award.

Summary

- **Simple sentences** are made up of only one clause.
- **Simple sentences** must have a subject and a verb.

Checking agreement

If you can identify the subject in a sentence, you will be able to check that you are using the correct form of the verb. This is known as **subject-verb agreement**. Look at the following sentences.

> She **was cycling** to school.
> They **were cycling** to school.

In the first sentence, the singular subject '**She**' agrees with the verb '**was**'. In the second sentence, the plural subject '**They**' agrees with the verb '**were**'.

A common mistake people make in their writing is to misuse the verbs **be** and **have**. The table below shows you the standard English forms for these words.

Subject	Verb		
	Have	Be (Present)	Be (Past)
I	have	am	was
he/she/it	has	is	was
we	have	are	were
you	have	are	were
they	have	are	were

Activity 1

Write out the standard English forms in the following sentences.

1 We **was** watching a film at the cinema.
2 They **was** in the library when we found them.
3 I **were** playing my guitar with my friends.
4 You **was** looking really embarrassed.
5 Billy **were** late for his lesson.

Checking subject-verb agreement

Subject-verb agreement can be tricky when the subject is made up of more than one word.

Tom and I **was playing** tennis.　**✗**
Tom and I **were playing** tennis.　**✔**

Subject-verb agreement can also be tricky when the subject is separated from the verb by another phrase.

Preeti and Tim, both of whom are good tennis players, **was helping** me with my serve.　**✗**
Preeti and Tim, both of whom are good tennis players, **were helping** me with my serve.　**✔**

Tips for checking subject-verb agreement

1 Identify the **subject** in the sentence.

2 Work out whether the subject could be replaced by any of these pronouns: **I**, **he**, **she**, **it**, **we**, **you** or **they**.

3 Read the sentence to yourself with the correct pronoun and make sure you have the verb that matches it, for example.

Tom and I were playing tennis.
　→ **We** were playing tennis.

Activity 2

Change the verb in **bold** in the following sentences so that the subjects and verbs agree.

1 The book that I was given by my parents **were** very good.

2 My cousins Ros and Melissa **was** dancing to the music.

3 The favourite of all Richard's hobbies **are** athletics.

4 My parents, who aren't mad at me anymore, **is** taking me to the cinema.

5 The plates, which crashed on the floor, **was** brand new.

6 Sam, who came shopping with us, **were** really good company.

7 Everyone, except Sarah and Maya, **were** going on the school trip.

Object

The **object** in a sentence usually comes after the verb. It tells you who or what is affected by the action described by the verb. In the following sentence, the volleyball is the object because it receives the punch.

> Jim punched the **volleyball**.

The object can be one word: a noun, or a pronoun. It can also be a group of words: a noun phrase.

> Matthew eats **a lot of rice pudding**.

Activity

Write out the following sentences and underline the **object**. Remember that the object can be one word or a group of words.

1 Mary dusted the shelves.
2 Take a break.
3 In October, I will celebrate my thirteenth birthday.
4 The next issue of the magazine will have more great bands.

Activity 2

Think of an **object** to complete the following sentences. Then write out the full sentences. Remember that the object can be one word or a group of words.

1 The chef prepared _____.
2 I photographed _____ at the zoo.
3 I would like _____ for my birthday.
4 In the newsagent's shop I bought _____.

Complement

The **complement** in a sentence usually comes after a verb. It usually gives more information about the subject.

> She became **a pilot**.

Complements are often nouns, noun phrases or adjectives.

Activity 3

Write out the following sentences and underline the **complement**.

1 The food tasted delicious.
2 She seemed a bit tired.
3 Their team were the winners.
4 Owen is my best friend.
5 The table looked rather dirty.
6 The pudding smelled wonderful.

Adverbial

The **adverbial** tells you **where**, **when**, **how** and **to what extent** something happened (as the examples in the box show). It can be a single word or a group of words.

Subject	Verb	Adverbial
Jo	went	to the funfair.
We	left	just after ten o'clock.
Samantha	danced	brilliantly.
The class	laughed	a lot.

Adverbials can also follow the object in the sentence.

James placed his bag **on the table**.

Activity 4

Write out the following sentences and underline the **adverbial**.

1 His brother cycled from home.
2 Charlie played the piano very well.
3 Ewan laughed vigorously.
4 We played basketball until dinnertime.
5 My best friend called me this morning.

Thinking back, moving forward

With your partner

— Write down the four rules used for identifying a sentence.
— Write a short play set in your school using the four main kinds of sentence.
— Explain to each other how to check subject-verb agreement.

On your own

How confident are you now that you can:
— identify a sentence
— use different kinds of sentence in your writing
— understand what a simple sentence is
— understand subject-verb agreement?

BUILDING SENTENCES

BUILDING SENTENCES

OBJECTIVES

This section will help you:

- build noun phrases
- understand how clauses are building blocks of sentences
- understand compound and complex sentences
- understand how to use connectives
- gain confidence in punctuating sentences.

Building simple sentences

A simple sentence contains one subject and one main verb.

> **She wore** a dress.
>
> subject   verb

However, simple sentences don't have to be short. It is possible to build them so that they have more detail.

> She wore **a dress**.
> She wore **a long black dress**.
> She wore **a long black dress with a red floral pattern on it**.

> I like **books**.
> I like **science-fiction books**.
> I like **classic science-fiction books**.
> I like **classic science-fiction books with lots of adventure**.

The words in **bold** in the sentences above are **noun phrases**. They act like a single noun and can be replaced by a pronoun.

Activity

Build the following simple sentences by adding detail to the nouns in **bold**.

1 **The clock** was ticking loudly.

2 **The teacher** walked into the classroom.

3 I like **music**.

Building noun phrases

You can make your writing more interesting by building **noun phrases**.

Activity 1

1 An author has just shown his editor the first few lines of his new children's ghost story. The editor said that she would like more detail in his writing.

Build **noun phrases** from the **bold** words below to create a more detailed picture for the reader. Use words that capture the atmosphere in this ghost story. For example:

> Thunder rumbled in **the darkening sky**.

2 Swap your writing with a partner. Check to see if the added words create a more detailed picture for the reader of this ghost story.

'Boo!'
'Don't scare me like that,' hissed Dan.
'Why?' teased Alice. 'Are you scared? It's only an empty house.'
Thunder rumbled in the **sky**.
Dan and Alice looked uneasily at the **house**. It stood at the top of a hill. They crept closer. There was no turning back now.
They reached the **gate**. A **cat** ran past, making Alice jump.
'Who's scared now?' joked Dan, nervously.

Clauses

Simple sentences have only one complete verb.

> I **ran** into the sea with my surfboard.
> It **was raining** outside.

In writing, you will see sentences that contain more than one complete verb. These are called **multiple sentences**. Examples of multiple sentences are **compound sentences** and **complex sentences**. We will visit these later in the book (pages 64–5 and 68–9).

> I **ran** into the sea with my surfboard then **swam** towards the waves.
> It **was raining** outside but we still **played** the match.

We need to know about **clauses** in order to understand how **multiple sentences** work.

What is a clause?

A **clause** is a group of words that has a complete verb. Clauses are the building blocks of sentences. Simple sentences have just one clause.

Multiple sentences have more than one clause.

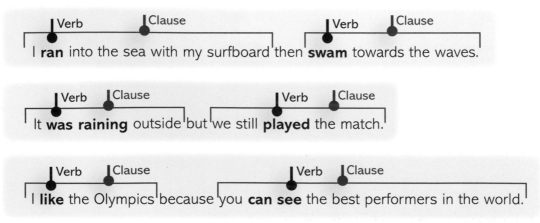

You can also identify multiple sentences because they often contain linking words.

┃linking word

I went to the theatre **and** watched a really good play.

Activity 1

Read the following extract from 'The New Boy' by Geddes Thomson.

The new boy was surrounded by a crowd of first years. He was a big broad-shouldered lad with sun-tanned face and dark curly hair. He was dressed in a fancy pullover and brown corduroys and he was wearing a tie. The first years seemed to be enjoying his company, because they were laughing and skipping about him like a pack of playful dogs.

Tom stopped and stared at the newcomer in *his* playground.

In pairs find:
- two examples of simple sentences
- two examples of multiple sentences.

Remember: simple sentences have only one clause and multiple sentences have more than one clause.

A helping hand:

Identify the **complete verbs** in each sentence.
- if there is **one complete verb**, it is a **simple sentence**.
- if there are **at least two complete verbs**, it is a **multiple sentence**.

Remember, verbs (or verb phrases) can be more than one word (see page 34).

Summary

- A **clause** is a group of words that has a complete verb. Clauses are the building blocks of sentences.
- A **simple sentence** has just one clause.
- A **multiple sentence** has more than one clause.

Compound sentences

What is a compound sentence?

Compound sentences are a type of multiple sentence. You get them by joining two simple sentences with words like **and**, **but** and **or**. For example:

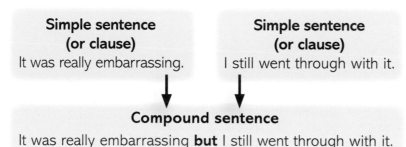

Simple sentence (or clause)	Simple sentence (or clause)
It was really embarrassing.	I still went through with it.

Compound sentence

It was really embarrassing **but** I still went through with it.

Activity 1

Make compound sentences by joining the simple sentences below. Use the linking words in the box.

and	**but**	**or**

1 Shreena could spend her pocket money now. She could save it for a rainy day.

2 I get the bus to school. I would rather ride my bike.

3 I sing lead vocal for the band. I play the guitar.

4 There are plenty of recycling facilities out there. Not everyone recycles.

5 You could take the stairs. You could take the escalator.

6 The house has three bedrooms. It has a garden.

7 I wanted to go swimming. The pool was closed.

8 Sami is good at science. He is good at art.

DID YOU KNOW?

Words that link sentences together such as **and**, **but** and **or** are called **connectives** or **conjunctions**.

What can go wrong?

Look at the sentence on the right.

The sentence is very long and tedious to read. It is easy to make compound sentences too long (like this example) by adding linking words such as **and** or **but**. Therefore, you must take care to avoid doing this in your writing.

I went to town and met my friends and I wanted a burger but we went for a pizza and then we went to the cinema and we saw a comedy film ...

Activity 2

The passage on the right was written by a student. It is made up of one sentence, which is too long! Improve the passage by splitting it into several shorter sentences. Where necessary:

- remove the words **and** and **but** (but don't make changes to the other words)
- change the punctuation (this includes changing lower case letters to capital letters).

I went to the zoo with my mum, dad and little brother Zach and we went straight to the monkey enclosure because monkeys are Zach's favourite, but I was desperate to go to see the lions but Mum and Dad said we should keep Zach happy and I didn't spend much time with the lions but it was still a great trip and I can't wait until we go again.

Connectives

What is a connective?

Connectives or **conjunctions** are **linking words**.
They are used to link simple sentences or clauses.
Using connectives allows us to extend our sentences.

Sentence or clause

I would love to go.

Sentence or clause

I've got netball practice
after school.

I would love to go **but** I've got netball practice after
school.   connective

Sentence or clause

Raza picked up
piles of books.

Sentence or clause

She arranged them
on the shelf.

Raza picked up piles of books **and** she arranged them
on the shelf.   connective

The connectives **and** and **but** are commonly used to link
simple sentences and clauses. However, there are many
useful connectives we can use in our writing to make it
more interesting. Look at the connectives below and what
they show.

Concession:	although	though	yet
Reason:	as	because	since
Result:	so		
Time:	after	then	since
	until	when	while
Condition:	if	unless	
Place:	where		

Activity 1

Select connectives from the box on the opposite page to fill in the gaps in the sentences below. Then write the sentences out in full. Try to use a different connective each time. The first one has been done for you.

1   The café was closed **so** we went to the pizza place instead.

2   My mum was angry _____ my music was loud.

3   You can have some ice cream _____ you finish your vegetables.

4   Jan and Philip were gossiping _____ the teacher was talking.

5   It has been raining _____ it is still pretty warm.

6   You won't be going out _____ you have finished your homework.

7   Our goalkeeper isn't here _____ we could use someone else for now.

8   Julian got a really good mark _____ he had arrived late for the test.

9   We put the tomato on the pizza base _____ we add the cheese.

10 We got a recycling bin _____ we started collecting glass and paper.

Reversing sentences

Look at the sentences you have written for Activity 1.
The connective joins two separate sentences.

Jan and Philip were gossiping **while** the teacher was talking.

It is possible to reverse the sentence, so that the sentence reads the other way round.

While the teacher was talking, Jan and Philip were gossiping.

Notice that there is now a comma between the two halves.

Activity 2

1   Look at the sentences you wrote for Activity 1 and see which ones can be reversed.

Complex sentences

What is a complex sentence?

Complex sentences are a type of multiple sentence.
They have more than one clause.

We didn't like the film.   It was scary.

We didn't like the film because it was scary.

Main and subordinate clauses

Complex sentences have a **main clause** and at least one **subordinate clause**.

A **main clause** can stand alone as a sentence as it expresses a complete thought.

Main clause	Main clause
We didn't like the film.	It was scary.

A **subordinate clause** doesn't express a complete thought. Therefore, it needs to be linked to a main clause.

Main clause	Subordinate clause
We didn't like the film	because it was scary.

This is another example:

Main clause	Subordinate clause
I read my book	while I was sitting in the launderette.

DID YOU KNOW?

A **main clause** is sometimes called an **independent clause** because it can stand on its own.

Activity 1

1   The clauses on the left below are **main clauses**. Each one needs matching with a **subordinate clause** on the right to make a **complex sentence**.

Find the clauses that match, and write them out as complete sentences.

1 The goalkeeper got struck by the ball	**a** unless you hurry up.
2 I wouldn't speak to him	**b** if my mum says that's OK.
3 I could stay at your house	**c** since starting karate classes.
4 We're not going to make it in time	**d** after I forgot Dad's birthday.
5 I have been feeling stronger	**e** although it is a nice day outside.
6 Ravi told me a joke	**f** when the striker took his shot.
7 I decided it was time to tidy my bedroom	**g** while swimming.
8 Mum made me fill in a calendar	**h** when I couldn't open my wardrobe door.
9 I looked at the horizon	**i** because I was upset.
10 We could stay in and watch a film	**j** until he apologised.

2   Look at the words that begin the subordinate clauses. What types of word are they?

More about clauses

In some sentences you will find the main clause at the beginning of the sentence. In other sentences you may find the main clause at the end of the sentence.

Look at the sentences below. The main clause is in **bold**.

She spilt sauce down her jumper while eating her spaghetti.

While eating her spaghetti, **she spilt sauce down her jumper.**

I couldn't face going back there after what I had said.

After what I had said, **I couldn't face going back there.**

We're going to the opening night of *Harry Potter*, if Dad gets the tickets.

If Dad gets the tickets, **we're going to the opening night of *Harry Potter*.**

Notice that a comma is used when the subordinate clause is at the beginning of the sentence.

Activity 1

Link the pairs of clauses on the opposite page to make **complex sentences**. You need to decide:

- which clause will be the subordinate one
- which connective to use
- where to put the connective.

For example:
The film had a scary scene. It frightened us.
Answers (the main clause is in **bold**):

- Because the film had a scary scene **it frightened us**.
- **The film had a scary scene** so it frightened us.
- When the film had a scary scene **it frightened us**.

These are the connectives you could use:

although	as	when	which
while	since	so	

1 I was walking up the stairs. I tripped over.

2 James counted to ten. Maya hid under the table.

3 I was with my friends. I felt really bored.

4 It was my birthday. We went to Alton Towers.

5 Will told us a secret. It made us gasp.

Activity 2

Swap your sentences with a partner. Between you, how many different sentences did you come up with?

Activity 3

Below is a letter from the advice page of a magazine. Rewrite the letter using some **complex sentences**. You need to:

- change some sentences to subordinate clauses
- use connectives.

For example:

> Since I have always been interested in unusual animals, I think I would like to keep an unusual pet at home.

These are the connectives you could use:

although	since	so	though

Dear Graham,

I have always been interested in unusual animals. I think I would like to keep an unusual pet at home. I already have a cat and a goldfish. I would like to keep more animals. I live in a three-bedroom house with my mum and young brother. It isn't too crowded.

I would like to know what you recommend. I am thinking of a snake or scorpion.

I look forward to hearing from you.

Yours sincerely,

Tom,

age 13

Sentences and how to stop them

A common mistake that students make in their writing is to join two clauses with a comma, rather than using a **connective** or separating them with a **full stop**. Using commas in this way can lead to sentences that are confusing. Take a look at the examples below.

> My sister **is allowed** to do work experience, she **is** older than me.   ✗
>
> My sister **is allowed** to do work experience. She **is** older than me.   ✔
>
> My sister **is allowed** to do work experience as she **is** older than me.   ✔

The main verbs in the examples above are underlined. If there is no **full stop** and no **connective** between two main verbs, check the punctuation very carefully.

Activity 1

In the following passage there are some commas where there should be full stops. Re-write the passage, changing **commas** to **full stops** where necessary. The main verbs are underlined.

> Haverstock <u>was</u> barely a village, it <u>was</u> a small and isolated place with a church, a shop, a few houses, a telephone box and a crossroads. There <u>was</u> a dried-up duck pond near the graveyard, with an old, ruined stocks by it.
>
> Charlotte <u>reached</u> into her pocket and <u>felt</u> for her phone. It <u>wasn't</u> there, it <u>must have fallen out</u> when she <u>had been running</u>. She <u>stopped</u> by the telephone box, maybe she <u>ought to call</u>, to tell someone where she <u>was</u>, just in case. But then she <u>realised</u> that the few coins she <u>had were</u> of no use; the payphone only <u>took</u> silver. She <u>didn't</u> even <u>think</u> to reverse the charges, she just <u>hurried</u> on.

Adapted extract from *Tins* by Alex Shearer

Activity 2

In the following passage there are again some commas where there should be full stops. The passage is more difficult to read than it needs to be because it is not divided up into sentences. In fact it goes on and on with just one full stop.

Rewrite the passage, changing **commas** to **full stops** where necessary.

Hint: each **new subject** will require a **new sentence** *unless* linked by a connective such as: *and, as, though.*

She walked on, it was a cold but clear country night, pale moonlight showed the way, her footsteps echoed and seemed at times to be pursuing her, then at other times to be slightly ahead of her, as though she was following them, hedges and brambles lined the fields, and twisted thorn trees writhed as if locked in pain, a faint, whispering breeze blew, full of murmuring.

Adapted extract from *Tins* by Alex Shearer

73

Looking at a text

Activity 1

Read the following start of an advertisement for
Rapid Rescue:

Can you believe it's happened again?

This will sound very familiar. You've got to get somewhere
urgently but your car doesn't start. Normally you'd start
shouting, crying or kicking your car.

However, time is passing whilst you're getting nowhere.

There is an alternative.

1 Find:
   - one question
   - one statement
   - one example of a simple sentence
   - one example of a compound sentence.

2 Explain why you think the author starts the
   advertisement with a question.

3 Explain why you think the author starts the main text
   with a statement.

4 Explain why you think the author chose to place
   the shortest sentence at exactly the point it is in the
   advertisement.

Activity 2

Read the following text by a student about fast food.

1 What kinds of sentences are being used?

2 Which sentences have the most impact on you when you read them?

3 Choose the sentence that you think is the most powerful. Be prepared to explain your choice.

How many of you have been to a fast food restaurant this week? Come on, don't be shy. Too many are doing this in Britain. There's no excuse for it. It's not the cheapest option, and I'm prepared to bet it's not the tastiest either. We all know the risks, but we shrug our shoulders and carry on blocking up our arteries and reducing the blood supply to our heart. Why not go to a healthier food store? Why not bring your own sandwiches? Don't do this to yourselves, people! Some of you reading this article, right now, could die as a result of your eating habits. Stop now. Cease this madness! The McDonalds salads are your enemies too. They're just as fattening, so don't be fooled by the advertising. We all know what's healthy and what's not, so let's do something about it.

4 Find examples of the following:
- a short sentence with a short dramatic message
- exclamations to add to the impact and emotion
- first person plural pronoun to involve the reader
- second person pronoun to involve the reader
- use of logical connectives to explain where the argument is leading
- use of questions to involve the reader.

Thinking back, moving forward

With your partner
Explain to each other:
- how can you create a compound sentence from two simple sentences
- how you can create a complex sentence from two simple sentences
- the difference between a compound sentence and a complex sentence.

On your own
How confident are you now that you can:
- build noun phrases
- understand how clauses are the building blocks of sentences
- create compound and complex sentences
- understand how to use connectives
- punctuate a sentence with confidence?

PARAGRAPHS AND WHOLE TEXTS

OBJECTIVES

This section will help you:

- understand the purposes of paragraphing
- gain confidence in arranging paragraphs
- understand how to link paragraphs
- plan the structure of your writing more effectively.

Using paragraphs

Have a look through a textbook or novel that your class is reading. Could you imagine how difficult it would be to follow if it was one long text?

You need to organise your text into **paragraphs** when you are writing more than a few sentences. **Paragraphing** is the process of organising your writing into groups of sentences to make it more cohesive. Paragraphs have the following advantages.

1 They help readers work their way through the text. When a text is in paragraphs, the reader has the option of pausing after a paragraph to think about what it is saying.

2 If the reader decides to break from reading before the end of the text, it is simpler for them to find their place when they return to it.

3 They show readers how the ideas are developing. When a new paragraph starts, it is a signal to the reader that the writer is moving from one stage of the text to another.

Look at the prologue opposite from *Artemis Fowl* by Eoin Colfer. It shows how well-planned paragraphs show a development in the ideas.

How does one describe Artemis Fowl? Various psychiatrists have tried and failed. The main problem is Artemis's own intelligence. He bamboozles every test thrown at him. He has puzzled the greatest medical minds and sent many of them gibbering to their own hospitals.

There is no doubt that Artemis is a child prodigy. But why does someone of such brilliance dedicate himself to criminal activities? This is a question that can be answered by only one person. And he delights in not talking.

Perhaps the best way to create an accurate picture of Artemis is to tell the by now famous account of his first villainous venture. I have put together this report from first-hand interviews with the victims, and as the tale unfolds you will realise that this was not easy.

In Paragraph 1, we are introduced to the protagonist, Artemis Fowl. We learn of Artemis's great intelligence.

In Paragraph 2, our picture of Artemis develops: we now learn that he is a criminal.

In Paragraph 3, the author signals to us that we will soon learn of Artemis's 'now famous' and intriguing tale.

You are now going to have a go at writing paragraphs for a text of your own.

Activity 1

Write three paragraphs describing a person you know, a character from a novel or film, or a fictional character or creature of your own creation, such as a monster.

Your writing

In this unit you will write an account of a place you know well. It will be aimed at people who might decide to visit this place. In your account, you need to give your readers a clear idea of what to do, what to see, and perhaps what to avoid.

Before you write your account, we will explore how you can organise your writing effectively in **paragraphs**.

Using and sequencing paragraphs

Read the extract from *Soul Surfer* by Bethany Hamilton.

(Note: some of the spellings and expressions are American.)

Paragraph 1

Having a home on a tiny island in the middle of the Pacific Ocean isn't for everybody. There are no big shopping malls, only a couple of movie theaters, no ice-skating rinks, no miniature golf or go-cart places. We have only one road to get around on, and if there is a traffic accident half the island can be blocked from getting anywhere for a long, long time.

Paragraph 2

It's such a small place that you get to know lots of people and can have friends all over the island. We always joke that if a kid gets in trouble in school, the parents know about it before the kid gets off the school bus. But the smallness also has its advantages: if your car breaks down on the side of the road, chances are good that someone you know will come by real soon and help out.

Paragraph 3

People who have lived their whole life in a big city don't always understand what my life here is like – or why I wouldn't want to, say, move to L.A. or New York or some other fast-paced city where there's lots of action and excitement. Here's what I think: you make your own adventure in life. And I truly believe that if you open your eyes to your surroundings, there's lots of neat stuff to be found practically anywhere on earth. For me, the grass is never greener outside of Hawaii.

Activity 1

Answer the following questions about the extract from *Soul Surfer*.

1 Which paragraph tells you:
  - about the road network
  - how easy it is to make friends
  - how far people help each other
  - what other people know about this place
  - what the writer's overall feelings are about the place
  - where the place is?

2 Give one of these labels to each paragraph:
  - opinions about the place
  - the people
  - the place.

3 Do you think these three paragraphs could be in any other order? Explain why you think the author chose this particular order.

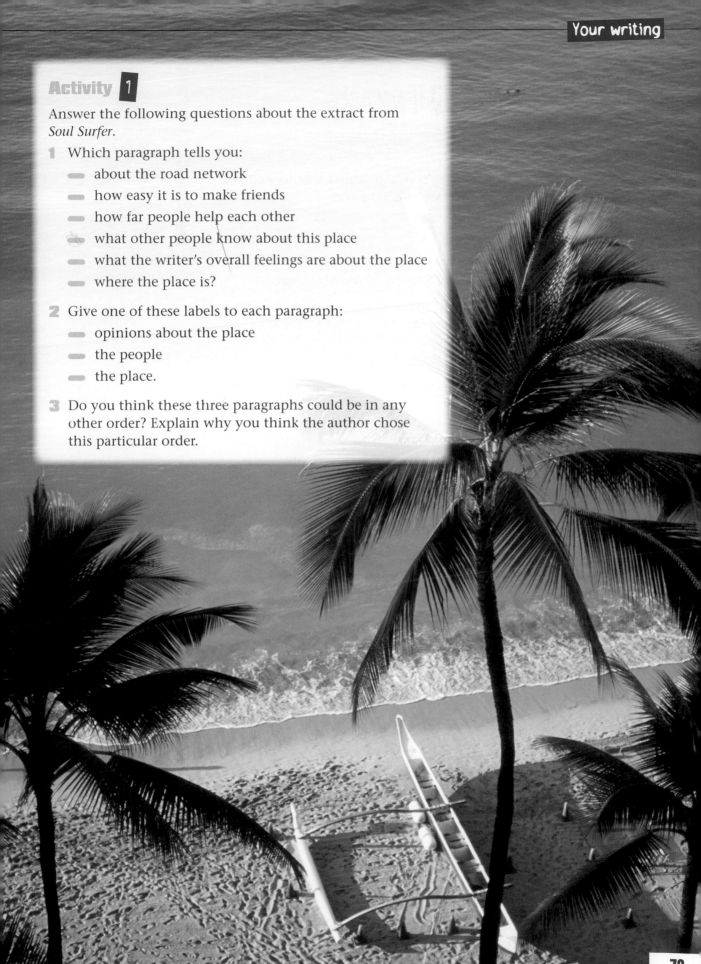

Organising your paragraphs

You could organise the paragraphs in your account in various ways. For example:

> **A** what your chosen place is like at different times of day and night
>
> **B** what different parts of your chosen place are like
>
> **C** what different kinds of opportunities and facilities are on offer.

Each of your paragraphs needs to focus on one topic only. You can use the first sentence in your paragraphs to indicate what that particular paragraph will be about.

DID YOU KNOW?

A **topic sentence** is usually the first sentence in a paragraph. It helps the reader follow the writer's train of thought.

Activity 2

Match the following paragraph starters to A, B or C above.

> **1** If you are looking for things to do in the morning …
>
> **2** The first thing you need to know is where you can stay.
>
> **3** What most people consider to be the centre and heart of … is ….

Now you are going to have a go at your own writing!

Activity 3

1 Write an account of a place you know well. It could be your home village, town or city, or a place you have visited, such as a holiday or day-trip destination. Imagine you are writing for a person who knows nothing about this place.

Use these notes to help you:

- Plan your paragraphs. Choose the topic that each of your paragraphs will be about, making sure that each of your paragraphs focuses on one topic only.

- Check that the order of your paragraphs is logical: the first paragraph should clearly be an opening and the last paragraph should clearly be an ending.

- Guide your reader through your writing by using **topic sentences**. For example:

  If you are looking for entertainment …
  In the centre of the town …
  When I first arrived in …

- Keep your reader interested in this place:

  - Use a strong opening and ending.

  - You could try using a **wide-shot paragraph** (where you give an idea of the overall look of the place) followed by a **close-up shot paragraph** (in which you describe a particular place in considerable detail).

  - Try to include senses apart from sight, such as smells and sounds.

2 Exchange your writing with a partner.
Tell your partner:

- at least one thing you think they have done well

- one particular way they could improve their writing.

Thinking back, moving forward

With your partner

- explain to each other the various reasons you can have for starting a new paragraph.

On your own

How confident are you now that you can:

- arrange a text in a logical order using appropriate paragraphs

- explain your reasons for choosing this sequence of paragraphs

- use appropriate topic sentences at the start of each paragraph, and group sentences together?

PUNCTUATION

OBJECTIVES

This unit will help you:

- know when and why to use capital letters
- know when and why to use full stops, commas, exclamation marks and question marks
- know when and why to use colons and semi-colons
- know when and why to use speech marks
- get the apostrophe in the right place every time.

Capital letters

Capital letters should be used for the following.

A To begin the first word in a sentence
The girl opened the book and studied the first page.

B Proper nouns: the name of a *particular* person, place or thing (see pages 12–13)
William Shakespeare, China, Google, *The Times*, Friday, Earth

C Adjectives based on proper nouns
Chinese, Irish, Shakespearean

D The personal pronoun 'I'
When I heard the post come through the letterbox, I ran to the door.

E To begin direct speech or a quotation
Vashti asked, 'Where was Tom yesterday?'

F Initials
BBC, J K Rowling, SE England, RSPCA

G Important words in titles (of people, books, films and organisations)
The Prince of Wales
Harry Potter and the Deathly Hallows
The Royal National College for the Blind

Activity 1

1 Write out the paragraph at the top of the next page using capital letters in the correct place.

2 For each capital letter you use, write down *why* you have used it, by matching it to one of A to G in the above list.

for the school trip last year, i went to the millennium centre in cardiff to see the play version of dickens's *nicholas nickleby*. this version was written by david edgar, and it was originally performed by the rsc in stratford-upon-avon. one critic said, 'this tremendous dickensian production was greeted by a spontaneous standing ovation.'

Deciding when to use a capital letter

Some words can have **either** a capital letter or not, such as **N**orth and **n**orth. When deciding whether to use a capital letter for these words, you need to look at how the words are being used. Below are two examples.

1 Use a capital letter for **N**orth, **E**ast, **W**est and **S**outh if they are names of areas of the country:

The **N**orth of England

Don't use a capital letter when you are writing about the compass direction of **n**orth, **e**ast, **w**est and **s**outh:

We drove **n**orth on the motorway.

2 Use a capital letter for **M**um, **D**ad, **A**untie, **U**ncle and so on, when they are used as names.

This morning **M**um asked me to wash the car.

When you are not referring to them as names, you don't use a capital letter.

This morning my **m**um asked me to wash the car.

DID YOU KNOW?

Capital letters are sometimes used for the first words in a newspaper report, for example: *A PROUD grandfather yesterday announced ...* They are also used to indicate that someone is speaking loudly: '*NO,*' *shouted Katie.*

Remember – if the word refers to a **particular** person, place or thing, start with a capital letter.

Activity 2

Use all you know about capital letters to make changes to the following passage.

my mum and i went to glasgow during the half-term holiday to see grandad. we haven't seen him in ages. i love hearing his scottish accent.

we took the train from bristol and travelled steadily north. the journey took ages. i read *harry potter and the philosopher's stone* by j k rowling to pass the time. we eventually arrived there in the early evening. when we got to grandad's house, mum called dad to say we had arrived safely.

Full stops, question marks and exclamation marks

There are three types of punctuation that can be used to end a sentence. Which one you use depends on the type of sentence.

Full stop	→	Statement	→	My winter jacket is blue.
Question mark	→	Question	→	What time is it?
Exclamation mark	→	Exclamation	→	What a noise!

Full stops

A **full stop** is used to end a sentence that is a statement:

It had rained for days.

Full stops should **not** be used after titles or headings in an information text.

Question marks

Question marks are used for **direct** questions.
For example:

- What is your favourite drink?
- Claire asked Tim, 'When would you like to meet up?'
- You are coming to the party, aren't you?

In the third example, a **tag question** has been added to the end of a statement. Tag questions can be used to put pressure on the person spoken to. In other words, a particular answer is expected!

Direct and indirect questions

Be careful when using question marks, as not all questions are direct questions. Notice the difference between **A** and **B** below.

  A 'Where are you going?' he asked.

  B He asked me where I was going.

In **A** the speech is **direct,** so a question mark is needed.
In **B** the question is described rather than asked directly,
so no question mark should be used. **B** is known as an
indirect question.
One way to work out if a sentence is a direct question is
to look at the position of the subject in the sentence.

- In direct questions, the subject is **after** the auxiliary verb:
  Are **you** going?

- In statements, the subject is **before** any auxiliary verb:
  He asked if **I** *was* going.

Exclamation marks

Exclamation marks are used to end sentences that express
a strong emotion such as excitement or anger, and when
someone says something forcefully:

Activity 1

Look at the following passage. Add full stops, question
marks and exclamation marks in the correct places.

The teacher asked me if I had read the latest Philip Pullman novel
  I asked, 'Which one is that'
  She named the book and I replied, 'Yes, I read it as soon as it came out
What a fantastic read'
  I asked if she'd enjoyed reading it
  She said yes, and added, 'Do you think the same central character might be
used again'
  I said I thought it would be a good idea, but asked if this could go on much
longer
  She replied, 'With a writer of that talent, there's no doubt that anything is
possible, don't you think'
  I agreed with her, exclaiming, 'No doubt at all'

Commas

Commas are used in the following ways.

A To separate the items in a list:

Her favourite sports are football, tennis, basketball and skating.

B To separate different adjectives:

His fingers were long, thin and crooked.

C To separate direct speech from the words that introduce or follow it:

Daniel said, 'I'll join you later.'

'That would be good,' I replied.

D After an adverb at the beginning of a sentence:

However, this was not the end of the story.

Activity 1

Write out the following sentences and put commas in the correct places. Indicate why the comma is being used in each case by writing **A**, **B**, **C** or **D**.

1 I would like some bananas apples oranges and mangoes.

2 Alison asked 'What if they don't turn up?'

3 It was a cold wet windy miserable day.

4 We visited places in England Scotland Ireland and Wales.

5 'That's really kind of you' I replied.

6 Secretly she crept into the room.

7 'I went to her house' I said quickly 'to apologise.'

Commas should also be used to separate different parts of a sentence.

a Use a comma to separate the subordinate clause from the main clause when the subordinate clause comes first.

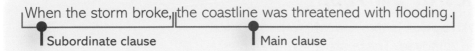

When the storm broke, the coastline was threatened with flooding.

Subordinate clause   Main clause

b Use a comma between each main clause when there is more than one in a sentence.

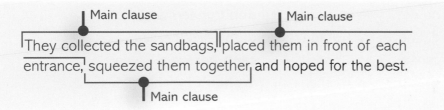

Main clause   Main clause

They collected the sandbags, placed them in front of each entrance, squeezed them together, and hoped for the best.

Main clause

c When a subordinate clause interrupts a main clause, there should be a comma on either side of it.

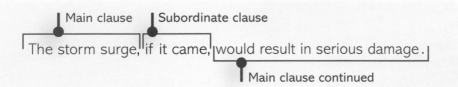

Main clause   Subordinate clause

The storm surge, if it came, would result in serious damage.

Main clause continued

Activity 2

Write out the following sentences, then add commas. Identify the reason behind using commas for each sentence by writing **a**, **b** or **c**.

1 After that terrible result the coach changed his training methods.

2 The referee having looked at the action replay decided not to award a penalty.

3 I rushed into the house took off my shoes hung up my jacket and sat down.

4 The result when the whistle was finally blown was a complete surprise.

5 Before leaving home I tried out my speech.

DID YOU KNOW?

Sometimes a comma can change the whole meaning of a sentence!

The talk was given by Veronica, who proved to be an expert on her dog and her cat.

(Veronica is an expert on her dog and her cat.)

The talk was given by Veronica, who proved to be an expert on her dog, and her cat.

(The talk was given by Veronica and her cat!)

Apostrophes

Apostrophes of omission

One use of **apostrophes** is to show where one or more letters have been removed. These are a few examples.

it is	→	it ~~i~~s	→	it's	**It's** too late to tell me that now.
it has	→	it ~~has~~	→	it's	**It's** been a really good day.
do not	→	do n~~o~~t	→	don't	I **don't** understand that.
did not	→	did n~~o~~t	→	didn't	I **didn't** like the film.
cannot	→	can~~no~~t	→	can't	I **can't** believe we won!
shall not	→	sha~~ll~~ n~~o~~t	→	shan't	We **shan't** be able to make it.

Activity `1`

Rewrite the sentences below. Use an apostrophe to shorten the words in bold.

1 I **did not** manage to see the film last night, so **I will** have to watch it next time **it is** on.

2 I **do not** think **you are** going to make it in time for the kick-off.

3 If I **cannot** open this jar, I **shall not** be having jam on my toast.

4 **It has** been really sunny today, so **we have** made a picnic for lunch.

Activity 2

Write out the following sentences in full. Replace the apostrophe with the missing letters. Underline the letter or letters that the apostrophe has replaced.

For example: *It **i**s time to start.*

1 **It's** time to get up.

2 **I'd** expected you to be more enthusiastic.

3 **There's** a programme on television tonight that **you'd** enjoy.

4 **Who'd** have predicted that result?

5 **You've** helped me make a good choice: **it's** been well worth reading that book.

Apostrophes of possession

Another use of the apostrophe is to show that something belongs to, or is associated with, something else.

For singular words, add **'s**:

> The dog that belongs to Graham → Graham**'s** dog
>
> An evening in winter   → A winter**'s** evening

For plural words ending in 's', just add **'**.

> The lesson for the students   → The student**s'** lesson
>
> The burrow of the rabbits   → The rabbit**s'** burrow

For plural words **not** ending in 's', add **'s**:

> The nursery for the children → The children**'s** nursery
>
> The suits for men   → The men**'s** suits

Notice that in each of the examples above, the apostrophe goes after the last letter of the version on the left.

Exception: **Possessive pronouns** don't use apostrophes:

> **his**   **hers**   **ours**   **yours**   **theirs**   **its**

> **DID YOU KNOW?**
>
> You do not use an apostrophe of possession with any pronoun except *one*:
> For example: *A room of one's own.*

Activity 3

Add **'s** to the following sentences so that they make sense.

1 Emily jumper is red.
2 We are going to Jamie house this afternoon.
3 Dad headache isn't getting any better.
4 I saw the article in yesterday newspaper.
5 Last night dinner was delicious.
6 We did some creative writing in Friday lesson.

Activity 4

Add **'s** or **'** to the following sentences so that they make sense.

1 The magicians tricks were fantastic!
(Note: there were three magicians.)
2 My aunt likes writing children stories.
3 Dad tried to find a present for Mum in the women clothing department.
4 The judges decision was final.
(Note: there were four judges.)

Common errors

A common mistake people make is to use apostrophes in plural words that don't need them.

Activity 5

Correct the following errors.

You should not use an apostrophe when:

- there are no missing letters
- the words are not showing that they own or are connected with anything.

Activity 6

Someone has crept into a secret meeting of scientists. They have written down the scientists' ideas to give them to a newspaper journalist. However, their use of apostrophes is not at all good!

Rewrite the ideas below, correcting the mistakes, so that they could appear in a newspaper. Be prepared to explain why you have made each change.

Idea 1: Before long, Spider Man suit's will exist that could make some young peoples' dreams come true. It will be possible to climb a skyscraper's vertical face.

Idea 2: Tiny hooks can be built into glove's so that they can grip a smooth surface such as glass. Each glove's designed to hold a mans weight or a womans weight. Two gloves could even hold two mens' weight or two womens' weight!

Idea 3: Its an idea based on a type of lizard called a *gecko*. A geckos hand has tiny hairs that help it cling to a smooth surface. But do'nt rush out and try to buy one just yet. They might be in the shop's in ten years' time.

Colons and semicolons

Colons

Colons are used for the following.

A To introduce a list of items:

To make this fruit smoothie you will need: a banana, an apple, a mango and some natural yoghurt.

B To separate two clauses in a sentence, when the second clause gives more information about the first:

Compasses are really useful: they help you to find your way.

C To introduce a quotation, saying or rule:

Remember what Grandma always says: an apple a day keeps the doctor away.

Activity 1

Write out the following sentences and put a colon in each one in the correct place. Indicate why the colon is being used in each case by writing **A**, **B** or **C** from the rules above.

1 As C P Scott said comment is free but facts are sacred.

2 I decided not to argue the friendship was more important.

3 My parents' shopping list included a barbecue, an outdoor table, some firelighters, and some sort of parasol for shelter from the sun.

4 The instructions fixed to the back of the rowing boat read no changing positions in the boat when away from the shore.

5 This lesson may be interrupted there is a visitor due.

6 To make a kite you need a light frame, some light but strong fabric and a long piece of string.

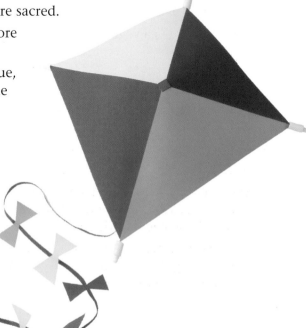

Semi-colons

Semi-colons are used for the following.

> **A To separate longer items in a list:**
>
>   I have visited: Paris, the capital of France; Cardiff, the capital of Wales; and Edinburgh, the capital of Scotland.
>
> **B To divide up long sentences:**
>
>   It wasn't just the swerve; it wasn't just the speed; each bounce zigzagged across the pitch as if the ball had a life of its own!
>
> **C To introduce a contrast:**
>
>   Some people like to go outside in the rain; others prefer to stay indoors.

In the case of **C**, the semi-colon could be replaced by a connective such as *but* or *while*.

Activity 2

Write out the following sentences and insert semi-colons where they are needed. Indicate why the semi-colon is being used in each case by writing **A**, **B** or **C** from the rules above.

1 He enjoys: playing the trombone football and rugby and any kind of martial art.

2 I eat meat he is a vegetarian.

3 The directions were clear but the mist made them impossible to follow.

4 Our team all had identical smart football kit their team were wearing t-shirts of roughly the same shade of green.

5 I ran to the bus stop I jumped on the bus I got off in town and I ran to the station.

6 You may use the sports hall on condition that you: remove outdoor shoes look after the equipment pay for any breakages and leave the place tidy.

7 The students behaved in different ways: some chatted to their neighbour some read a book while others got ahead with their homework.

> **DID YOU KNOW?**
>
> Instead of using a **semi-colon** for a contrast, you can use a **conjunction** such as although, but, while:
> I eat meat; he is a vegetarian.
> I eat meat, **but** he is a vegetarian.

Speech marks and inverted commas

Punctuation of speech

When characters speak in a cartoon, we see the words they are saying inside speech bubbles.

In writing, we use **speech marks " "** instead of speech bubbles:

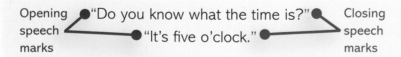

Opening speech marks ——→ "Do you know what the time is?" ——→ Closing speech marks
"It's five o'clock." ——→

Activity 1

Write out the following sentences.
Add the missing speech marks.

1 What time are we meeting today?

2 I found your bag.

3 I can't believe we won!

4 There they are.

5 Do you want to watch a film?

DID YOU KNOW?

When writing by hand you are likely to use " and " for speech marks. However, when writing using a computer, it is common to use ' and ' instead.

Rules for punctuating speech

There are certain rules you should follow when punctuating speech in a piece of writing.

Read the following extract and the annotations.
Then complete Activity 2.

> Speech starts on new line with opening speech marks and a capital letter.

> End speech with a comma if it isn't the end of the sentence.

> Don't start a new paragraph if the same person is speaking.

> End speech with a full stop and closing speech marks if it's the end of the sentence.

> Start a new paragraph when a new person speaks.

> You can end speech with a question mark or exclamation mark, with the same sentence continuing afterwards.

The policewoman put a jacket round her and sat in the back with the woman, and they drove off through the little town.

"Here," said the woman, passing her a sandwich. "Peanut butter. Hope you like it. It's all I've got."

"It's all she's ever got," said the policeman from the front. She'd put peanut butter in her coffee if she could."

The policewoman laughed.

"Never mind him," she said to Jess. "He's got no taste. You go ahead and eat."

"Thank you." She hated peanut butter but she ate the sandwich gratefully. "What time is it?" she said dully.

"Nine o'clock," said the policewoman.

Nine o'clock.

She'd been in the water about eleven hours. People had swum the Channel in that time. She stared out of the window, unsure what to feel.

The policewoman was passing on a message to the hospital.

"She's fine," she was saying, "just tired and cold."

Extract from *River Boy* by Tim Bowler

> Don't use a capital when restarting speech within the same sentence. But use a comma before the speech marks.

Activity 2

The following extract is about Jess, who has just completed a long swim. Match up the numbered circles in the extract to the rules shown below.

The policewoman put a jacket round her and sat in the back with the woman, and they drove off through the little town.

"❶ Here, ❷" said the woman, passing her a sandwich. "❸Peanut butter. Hope you like it. It's all I've got. ❹"

"❺ It's all she's ever got," said the policeman from the front. She'd put peanut butter in her coffee if she could."

The policewoman laughed.

"Never mind him," she said to Jess. "He's got no taste. You go ahead and eat."

"Thank you." She hated peanut butter but she ate the sandwich gratefully. "What time is it? ❻ " she said dully.

"Nine o'clock," said the policewoman.

Nine o'clock.

She'd been in the water about eleven hours. People had swum the Channel in that time. She stared out of the window, unsure what to feel.

The policewoman was passing on a message to the hospital.

"She's fine," she was saying, "❼ just tired and cold."

Extract from *River Boy* by Tim Bowler

A A question mark or exclamation mark at the end of speech **acts like a comma**, with the same sentence continuing after it.

B **Don't** use a capital letter when speech restarts **in the same sentence**. **Do** use a comma before the speech marks.

C Don't start a new paragraph if the same person is still speaking.

D End speech with a comma and then close the speech marks if it **isn't** the end of the sentence.

E End speech with a full stop and closing speech marks if it **is** the end of the sentence and the end of the speech.

F Start a new paragraph the first time someone speaks. Use opening speech marks and a capital letter.

G Start a new paragraph when a **different** person speaks.

Activity 3

Write out the sentences below and add the speech marks in the correct places.

1 I can smell trouble, said Daniel.

2 Look at that! shouted Ned.

3 Everyone looked really miserable, said Jo.

4 What are we going to do now? cried Philip.

5 We went without you, said Lisa, because we didn't think you were going to turn up.

6 I don't understand, said David. It doesn't make sense.

DID YOU KNOW?

A comma sits **outside** the speech marks when just a few words are being quoted. For example:

Katie said that it was 'fantastically sunny there', which is the opposite of here!

Activity 4

The writer of the following extract hasn't used speech marks and hasn't laid out the text correctly. Write out the extract using correct punctuation and layout.

Mum, Samuel and Lucy had arrived at the theme park. Mum, mum, let's go on Megaphobia first, screamed Samuel. No – the pirate ship mum, yelled Lucy. Mum tried to calm them by saying, It's all right, we'll go on both. Can we buy the photo? Lucy interrupted. Please, please Mum! Perhaps, she replied, if you stop shouting and interrupting!

Activity 5

1 Imagine a new student arrives at your school and is concerned about settling in. You reassure them and explain some of the good things about the school.

Write the conversation. Try to show in your writing that you have understood all the rules.

2 Exchange your writing with a partner. Check that your partner has used all the rules correctly.

Thinking back, moving forward

With your partner

- Discuss all the times when you should use capital letters and why.

- Explain to each other how to make sure you use the apostrophe correctly every time.

On your own

How confident are you now that you can:

- use full stops, commas, colons and semi-colons correctly

- punctuate speech accurately?

COMMON ERRORS

This unit will help you:

- understand why certain common errors are made
- learn strategies to avoid making these errors.

Would/Should/Could have

What can you find in common in all the following words?

Could've	**Should've**	**Would've**

The three words above include shortened forms of the word '**have**':

I could **have** walked   I should **have** walked.
I would **have** walked.

A common mistake is to write the word '**of**' instead of '**have**'. This could be because the letters **'ve** sound like the word '**of**'.

I could **of** walked.   ✗

Remember: the word '**have**' is a **verb** and the word 'of' is not. You shouldn't use 'of' as a verb:

I will **of** done it by tomorrow.   ✗
I will **have** done it by tomorrow.   ✔

Activity 1

In the sentences below '**of**' and '**have**' are sometimes used incorrectly. Write the sentences correctly, writing out in full any words with apostrophes.

1 I might of been wrong to say it.
2 We could've been at the front if we'd been here earlier.
3 They should of listened to our advice.
4 We should've stayed to the very end.
5 If we'd trained more we would've been in the team.
6 I could of told you the result before it started.
7 You couldn't of been reading the right books.
8 I *could've* been there and I *should've* been there.

You're/Your

Sometimes '**you're**' and '**your**' get confused because they sound the same.

You're is the shortened form of '**you are**':

You are early today. → **You're** early today.

Your means something belonging or relating to you:

Where is **your** coat?

The door is just on **your** right.

Activity 2

Look at each of the following sentences and decide whether the word **your** or **you're** should fill in the gap. Write out the sentences correctly.

1 _____ report seems to have improved.

2 They're certain _____ the best person for the job.

3 We're going to have to see if _____ up to the challenge.

4 _____ going to have to give up _____ position in the queue.

Who's/Whose

Sometimes '**who's**' and '**whose**' get confused because they also sound the same.

This is where you would use the word **whose**:

1 In a question, to ask 'belonging to whom?'

Whose bike were you riding yesterday?

2 In a sentence, to mean 'of whom' or 'of which'.

I can't remember **whose** name was on the letter.

Who's is short for **who is** or **who has**:

Who is going first?　　　→　**Who's** going first?
Who has eaten my cake?　→　**Who's** eaten my cake?

Activity 3

Fill in the gaps in the following sentences with either **who's** or **whose** so that they make sense.

1 _____ there?

2 _____ is this coat?

3 I had to decide _____ advice to follow.

4 _____ eaten all the rice pudding?

5 _____ sister did you say you saw?

STRATEGY

To avoid misusing '**who's**', read out the words in full and see if the sentence still makes sense. Read '**who's**' as '**who is**' or '**who has**'.

There/Their/They're

There, **their** and **they're** are often misused as they all sound the same, but they all mean different things.

There

There means 'in that place' or 'at that place':

> The house is just **there**.   I want to travel **there**.
> I was **there** yesterday.   **There's** my pen.

There is also used in statements:

> **There** is a good film on television tonight.

Their

Their means 'belonging to them' or 'relating to them':

> **Their** time on the rollercoaster was up.
> I liked to listen to **their** opinions.

STRATEGY

To avoid misusing the word '**their**', replace it with the words '**her and his**' to see if the sentence still makes sense.

They're

They're is the shortened form of '**they are**':

> **They are** going for a walk.
> **They're** going for a walk.

STRATEGY

To avoid misusing '**they're**', read out the words in full and see if the sentence still makes sense. For example, you would read '**They're** just joking' as '**They are** just joking'.

Activity 4

Select the word **there**, **they're** or **their** for the spaces below, so that each sentence makes sense. Then write out the sentences in full.

1 _____ going to miss _____ train.

2 _____ was early morning mist on the lake.

3 On _____ team _____ were three newcomers.

4 When they've left, _____ going to be difficult to replace.

5 _____ definitely going to have to get _____ act together if _____ going to get _____ that early.

Too/To

Too and to often get confused.

Too

Too means 'excessively'.

There is **too** much to do today!

Too also means 'as well'.

Are you going to the party **too**?

In these cases the *oo* sound is similar to the *oo* sound in 'zoo'.

To

To can be used as a preposition meaning 'in the direction of'.

We went **to** the library.

To can also sit in front of a verb.

I would like **to** go swimming.

Notice that the sound of the word '**to**' is different from '**too**'. You can avoid misusing the word '**to**' by checking that the word '**too**' doesn't apply in the sentence.

> **DID YOU KNOW?**
>
> In colloquial English, '**too**' can also mean 'very': Mandy won't be **too** pleased if we are late. I'm not feeling **too** well.

> **DID YOU KNOW?**
>
> When the word '**to**' sits in front of a verb, the verb is in its 'infinitive form'.

Activity 5

Write out the following sentences, using either **to**, or **too** in the spaces so that each sentence makes sense.

1 The cyclists rode _____ fast for their own safety.

2 I have _____ tell you that sounds just _____ good _____ be true.

3 There was _____ little evidence _____ make a trial possible.

4 I'm planning _____ go _____ the cinema tonight.

5 _____ reach their goal, they had _____ face up _____ their inner fears and doubts.

Where/Were/We're

Where, **were** and **we're** may not sound the same, but they still get confused easily.

Where

Where is used in questions when we are asking about a place.

Where is my bag?   **Where** can I find the travel books?

Where did Gareth go?   **Where** did you park the car?

Where is also used to link different parts of the sentence to show how they are connected.

That is the **stadium where the team won the match**.

Were

The verb **to be** is irregular. In the past tense it is as follows:

Past tense
I/he/she/it **was**
we/you/they **were**

What **were** you saying?

They **were** catching a train to Cardiff.

We're

We're is the shortened form of '**we are**'.

We're going to perform a play.

Activity 6

Write out these sentences, inserting **where**, **we're** or **were** in the spaces so that the sentences make sense.

1 Could you please let me know when _____ close to _____ we need to get off the bus?

2 _____ _____ you when we needed you?

3 _____ on our way – I have no idea _____!

4 _____ you planning to leave early to get to the place _____ going to?

5 If you _____ right, _____ nearly _____ we need to get to.

STRATEGY

To avoid misusing '**we're**', read out the words in full and see if the sentence still makes sense. For example, you would read '**We're** just joking' as '**We are** just joking'.

You and me/You and I

A mistake that writers and speakers often make is confusing '**me**' and '**I**':

Danny told **I** a secret. ✗
Danny told **me** a secret. ✔

	Subject pronoun	Object pronoun	
First person	I	me	
Second person	you	you	singular
Third person	she/he/it/one	her/him/it	
First person	we	us	
Second person	you	you	plural
Third person	they	them	

These are the rules for using the correct word:

Rule 1:

Look at the table above. Then:
- use the **subject pronoun** for the **subject** of the verb
- use the **object pronoun** for the **object** of the verb.

Rule 2:

Use the **object pronoun** after a preposition.
(Prepositions are words such as *to*, *after*, *between*, *for* and *with*.) For example: To **me**, it looks as if it will rain.

Activity 7

Discuss which rule is being applied for the pronoun in **bold** in each of the following sentences.

1 I told **her**.
2 To **me**, it seems cold in here.
3 Daniel asked **him**.
4 I closed the door after **me**.
5 I heard the news through **them**.
6 She went to the film with James and **me**.
7 Rachel and **I** were playing tennis.
(Tip: the subject can be more than one word.)

Thinking back, moving forward

With your partner
- Make a leaflet advising students how to avoid common errors in their writing.

On your own
How confident are you now that you can:
- understand why certain common errors are made
- use strategies to avoid making these errors?

APPLYING YOUR LEARNING

Speaking and listening task

Your task is to prepare a speech to the class about a modern gadget or consumer item that *you* think should *not* have been invented. You must persuade the class that you are right! The rest of the class might have the opportunity to question you before your choice is put to the vote.

For example, there is a jacket on the market for children with built in GPS (global positioning system) so that parents know where their children are. It costs £250 to buy, but you also pay a £10 monthly charge.

Use the following list to help you.

- You can use the jacket example mentioned here, or another real example, or one you have made up.

- You should organise your speech, for example:
  - what the product is
  - who the product is aimed at
  - why the inventors may believe it is useful
  - why you disagree
  - your persuasive conclusion to convince the class you are right!

- You can be relatively informal in your speech (for instance, using colloquial words such as *gizmo*), but you should still aim to use standard English most of the time.

- Use some ideas you have gained from this grammar book, as well as making an original selection of words.

Grammatical suggestions you could include

- **Adjectives:** annoying, expensive, hideous, pointless, ridiculous, useless …
- **Nouns:** customer, gadget, gimmick, gizmo, invention, people, person, product, purpose + proper name for product.
- **Pronouns:** anybody, anyone, everybody, everyone, nobody, no one, nothing, I, someone, themselves, you, yourself …
- **Verbs:** to buy, to claim, to choose, to convince, to deceive, to invent, to persuade, to select, to sell, to trick, to waste …
- **Adverbs:** absolutely, completely, entirely, presumably, purely, ridiculously, uselessly, wrongly …
- **Connectives for compound sentences:** and, but, or.
- **Connectives for complex sentences:** although, because, if, unless, since, so …
- **Statements:** e.g. It costs £250.
- **Rhetorical questions:** e.g. What is the point of this gadget?
- **Exclamations:** e.g. It's amazing to think anyone would pay this much!
- **Directives (using imperatives):** e.g. Don't waste your money on this. Stop and think.

Reading task

Read the following newspaper article, then answer the questions that follow. You will need to know that the *Mary Celeste* was a boat that was found, more than 100 years ago, drifting without its crew. This article is about a much more recent boat.

THE TIMES Saturday 21 April 2007

Mystery of 'Mary Celeste' yacht

► Boat found adrift off Australian coast

► Crew missing but no sign of difficulty

Bernard Lagan
Sydney

The table was set. Laptop screens flickered in the cabin and mobile phones and sunglasses were on the chart table in front of the empty chairs. But there was no crew.

'It's almost like they just stepped off the boat,' said Trevor Wilson, pilot of the rescue helicopter sent to investigate after the catamaran was spotted drifting off the Queensland coast.

The discovery of the *Kaz II* without her three-man crew has mystified Australian rescue teams. Other than a ripped sail, everything seemed perfectly normal. The engine idled in neutral and the marine radio was on. Three wallets were on the table.

Her emergency equipment, including life jackets and the emergency locator beacon, appeared not to have been touched. The dinghy was still lashed to the hull.

By late yesterday 12 aircraft and four vessels were searching 4,000 sq nautical miles for the three men who set out on Sunday from Airlie Beach in North Queensland. An Australian Army Black Hawk helicopter was expected to join the search today.

The *Kaz II* was spotted by a coastal patrol aircraft on Wednesday 200km (125 miles) north of her departure point, drifting in calm seas. Because the patrol could not make radio contact with the catamaran or see anybody aboard, a rescue helicopter was sent out on Thursday and a crewman winched down.

By chance, a television crew from the Australian Broadcasting Corporation was on the helicopter making a documentary about the rescuers' work. Their footage was broadcast last night. The director, Jan Catoni, said: 'There was concern for the safety of the rescue officer who was winched down because he was boarding a vessel by himself. We had no sense of what he might find.'

Footage shows him emerging from the cabin eventually with his arms outstretched and palms turned upward to indicate that nobody was aboard.

There were no plausible theories last night to explain why the crew might have disappeared.

Questions

1 In paragraph 1 the journalist uses the **adjectives** 'empty' and 'no'. Explain whether you think these were good choices of adjectives and why.

2 In paragraph 2 the journalist quotes the pilot of the rescue helicopter: 'It's almost like they just stepped off the boat.'

   a Who does the **pronoun** 'they' refer to?

   b Why do you think the journalist doesn't say exactly who 'they' are at this point?

3 In paragraph 3 the journalist uses the **verb** 'mystified'. Explain whether you think this is a good choice of verb and why.

4 List all the words in paragraph 5 which start with a **capital letter**, apart from words at the beginning of sentences. Explain why a capital letter is used in each case.

5 Explain why you think the journalist chose to start his article with a short **simple sentence**, *The table was set.*

6 In paragraph 1, why do you think the journalist did not combine the second and third sentences into a longer **compound sentence**? This might have looked like this:
Laptop screens flickered in the cabin and mobile phones and sunglasses were on the chart table in front of the empty chairs, but there was no crew.

7 Find one complex sentence in paragraph 6 or 7. (Find a sentence that includes a connective other than *and*, *but* or *or*.)

8 Why do you think the journalist chose to use a **complex sentence** in this case?

9 Explain why a **colon** is used in paragraph 7.

10 Explain why you think 'Mary Celeste' is in inverted commas in the headline.

11 In paragraph 8 the journalist writes:
Footage shows him [the rescue officer] emerging from the cabin eventually with his arms outstretched and palms turned upward to indicate that nobody was aboard.
What does the choice of the **adverb** 'eventually' suggest?

12 In the final paragraph the journalist uses the **adjective** 'plausible'. Explain what you think this adjective means in this context.

Writing task

Write an article for a newspaper explaining why your favourite town or city is the ideal location for the next Olympic Games.

Read the list below to help you.

- Start your article with a suitable headline.
- Try to make use of a variety of sentence types, such as *statements*, *questions* and *exclamations*, and a variety of sentence patterns including *simple*, *compound* and *complex* sentences.
- Remember this is a *persuasion* text rather than a *recount* text.

You could use some of the following grammatical suggestions, but make your own choices too. Use some ideas you have gained from this book, including making an original selection of words and using a range of sentence patterns.

Grammatical suggestions you could include

- **Prepositions of time:** after, before, during, on, throughout, to, until ...
- **Nouns:** bus, car, train, plane, athletics, basketball, football, judo, karate, skiing, swimming, etc. + proper nouns for particular people and places.
- **Pronouns:** we, you, they ...; ourselves, yourselves, themselves; everybody, everyone, everything, nobody, no one ...
- **Verbs:** to arrive, to celebrate, to enjoy, to experience, to meet, to perform, to watch ...
- **Adjectives:** amazing, breathtaking, exciting, impressive, magnificent, successful, unique, unrivalled ...
  - comparatives: better, more (attractive, etc.)
  - superlatives: best, most (friendly, etc.).
- **Adverbs:** brilliantly, definitely, genuinely, marvellously, safely, undoubtedly ...
- **Connectives for compound sentences:** and, but, or.
- **Connectives for complex sentences:** after, as, because, before, by, during, since, so, so that, until, while, ...

Heinemann is an imprint of Pearson Education Limited, a company incorporated in England
and Wales, having its registered office at Edinburgh Gate, Harlow, Essex, CM20 2JE.
Registered company number: 872828

www.heinemann.co.uk

Text © Pearson Education Limited 2008

First published 2008

12 11 10 09
10 9 8 7 6 5 4 3 2

British Library Cataloguing in Publication Data is available from the British Library on request.

ISBN 978 0 43522 48 75

Designed by Ken Vail Graphic Design
Produced by Bigtop Design Limited
Original illustrations © Pearson Education Limited, 2008
Illustrated by Adrian Barclay (c/o Beehive Illustration) – pages 46, 47; Seb Burnett – pages 11, 13, 30, 35, 58, 68,
70, 100; Seb Camagajevac (c/o Beehive Illustration) – pages 19, 41, 61, 73, 77; Phil Healey – pages 5, 10, 16,
18, 24, 32, 40, 44, 48; Peter Lubach – pages 7, 21, 20, 88, 94, 99; Dusac Pavile (c/o Beehive Illustration) pages
53, 91; Daria Petrilli - page 33, 56; Francois Ruyer (c/o Beehive Illustration) page 9; Rupert Van Wyke (c/o Beehive
Illustration) pages 37, 97.
Cover design by Ken Vail Graphic Design
Cover illustration by Martin Aston (Just for Laffs)
Printed in China (EPC/02)

Acknowledgements

The author and publisher would like to thank the following individuals and organisations for permission to reproduce
photographs: p13 (pumpkin) © Lorthios/photocuisine/Corbis; p13 (kangaroo sign) © istockphoto/Karen Moller; p13
(shoe) © Mike Blake/Reuters/Corbis; p25 © istockphoto/Steeve Roche; p26 © istockphoto/Elena Schweitzer; p29 ©
istockphoto/Graeme Whittle; p54 © Roland Weihrauch/epa/Corbis; p65 © Nicole Duplaix/National Geographic/Getty
Images; p74 © istockphoto; p79 © Douglas Peebles/Corbis; p80 © Neale Clark/Robert Harding World Imagery/Corbis;
p86 © Richard Hutchings/Corbis; p90 (bananas) istockphoto/christine balderas; p90 (potatoes) istockphoto/John
Steele; p90 (tomatoes) istockphoto/angel rodriguez; p92 © Dorling Kindersley/Getty Images.

Every effort has been made to contact copyright holders of material reproduced in this book. Any omissions will be
rectified in subsequent printings if notice is given to the publishers.
Headline and small extract of text from 'Why gangs of youths buzz off when they hear the hum of a Mosquito', *The
Times*, 21 April 2007. © NI Syndication Limited 2007. Reprinted with permission; extract from *Stormbreaker* by
Anthony Horowitz, published by Walker Books © Anthony Horowitz. Reprinted by permission of The Peters Fraser
& Dunlop Group Limited on behalf of Anthony Horowitz; extracts from *Tins* by Alex Shearer, published by Macmillan.
Reprinted with permission of Macmillan Children's Books; words from Cadbury's chocolate wrappers. © Cadburys.
Reprinted with permission; tiny extracts from an Alton Towers advert. Reprinted with the kind permission of Alton
Towers; tiny extract 'Everyone likes a challenge', Crown Copyright materials reproduced with permission of the
controller of the HMSO; extract from *George's Marvellous Medicine* by Roald Dahl, published by Jonathan Cape Ltd
and Penguin Books Limited. Reprinted with permission of David Higham Associates; short extract from 'The New Boy'
by Geddes Thomson. Reprinted with the kind permission of Lucy Thomson; extract from *Artemis Fowl* by Eoin Colfer,
(Viking 2001) Copyright © Eoin Colfer, 2001. Reprinted with permission of Penguin Books UK; extract from *Soul
Surfer* by Bethany Hamilton with Sheryl Berk and Rick Bundschuh. Copyright © 2004 by Bethany Hamilton. Reprinted
with the permission of MTV Books/Pocket Books, a division of Simon & Schuster Inc; short extract from *River Boy* by
Tim Bowler, published by OUP 2006. Copyright © Tim Bowler 1997. Reprinted by permission of Oxford University
Press; article 'Mystery of Mary Celeste yacht' by Bernard Lagan, *The Times*, Saturday 21 April 2007. Copyright © N I
Syndication Limited, 21 April 2007. Reprinted with permission.